THE SERMON ON THE MOUNT

FIRST EDITION . . *December, 1896.*
Reprinted in the same month
Reprinted . . . . January, 1897.
Reprinted . . . . . March, 1897.
Reprinted . . . . . June, 1897.
Reprinted . . . . March, 1898.
Reprinted . . . December, 1898.
Reprinted . . . . . June, 1900.
Reprinted . . . . . October, 1901.
Reprinted . . . . . October, 1902.
Reprinted . . . . January, 1905.

Edition (6d.) for distribution in paper covers, March, 1904.
Reprinted . . . . October, 1904.
Reprinted . . . . March, 1906.
SECOND EDITION (1/-) . . . . *June, 1910.*

THE SERMON ON THE MOUNT

A PRACTICAL EXPOSITION

BY CHARLES GORE, D.D., D.C.L., LL.D.

BISHOP OF BIRMINGHAM

LONDON

JOHN MURRAY, ALBEMARLE STREET, W.

1910

PRINTED BY
HAZELL, WATSON AND VINEY, LD.,
LONDON AND AYLESBURY.

PREFACE TO THE REISSUE OF 1910

In reissuing this little book in a new form I wish, by way of preface, to say a few words upon the passages (pp. 72–78 and Appendix III., p. 227) in which I deal with the question of divorce in the Christian Church. I am not prepared to alter the conclusions there drawn, so far as they were drawn from the first Gospel, upon which alone I was commenting. But I should wish to express a different opinion on the relation of the statements about divorce in the first Gospel to those given us by St. Mark and St. Luke.

The course of recent criticism seems to make it fairly certain that we must regard the Gospels of St. Mark and St. Luke as giving us our Lord's teaching on this subject in its original form. They are as follows :

St. Mark x. 11, 12 : " And he saith unto

them, Whosoever shall put away his wife,
and marry another, committeth adultery
against her : and if she herself shall put
away her husband, and marry another,
she committeth adultery."

St. Luke xvi. 18 : "Every one that
putteth away his wife and marrieth another, committeth adultery : and he that
marrieth one that is put away from a
husband committeth adultery."

Cp. 1 *Cor.* vii. 10, 11 : "But unto the
married I give charge, yea not I, but the
Lord, That the wife depart not from her
husband (but and if she depart, let her
remain unmarried, or else be reconciled
to her husband) ; and that the husband
leave not his wife."

Our Lord in these passages is represented as recognizing remarriage after
divorce in no case at all. He treats
marriage as strictly indissoluble. The
astonishment of the disciples as expressed
even in the first Gospel (St. Matt. xix. 10 :
"If the case of the man is so with his wife,
it is not expedient to marry ") seems to
require this teaching to make it intelligible. It would not be intelligible if our
Lord were only reasserting the stricter of
two views about divorce already current

among the Jews.[1]   On the other hand, it
is certain that the passages in the first
Gospel upon which I have commented in
the text of this book do admit an exception to the indissolubility of marriage in
favour at least of the innocent husband
in the case of his wife's adultery.   I
must adhere to all that is said in this book
in support of this conclusion ; but I now
find myself constrained to believe that
the exception as recorded in St. Matthew,
though it is an integral part of our present
Gospel, represents a serious modification
of our Lord's teaching, due probably to
Jewish tradition within the Church.   The
Jewish Christians seem to have intro-
duced a gloss into their record of our
Lord's teaching, believing, no doubt, that
they were rightly interpreting His mind ;
and the gloss is represented in our first
Gospel.   The fact that the Christian
Church has accepted the first Gospel, and
stamped it with the fullest authority,
accounts for the teaching of the Church
on the indissolubility of the marriage tie
having been in certain times and places

[1] Also the alteration of the original question (St. Mark
x. 3), " Is it lawful for a man to put away his wife ? "
by the addition of the words " for every cause " (Matt.
xix. 3) is most significant.

1*

uncertain. We cannot to-day equitably
ignore the appeal to the first Gospel, even
though we do not believe it to represent
on this point the original teaching of our
Lord. My practical conclusions therefore are not different from those set out
in this book, except that I should now be
still more decisive than formerly in resisting any proposal to introduce any exception into the existing law of the Church
in England.

For the substance of this note—so far
as it concerns the Gospels—I would refer
to Dr. Plummer's *Exegetical Commentary
on St. Matthew* (Elliot Stock) and Allen's
*International Critical Commentary on St.
Matthew* (T. & T. Clark), on Matt. v. 31 ff.
and xix. 3 ff. Also to Dr. Salmon's
Human Element in the Gospels (Murray,
1907), p. 391, and to a work of Professor
Tyson's entitled *The Teaching of our Lord
as to the Indissolubility of Marriage* (Uni-
versity Press of Sewanee, Tennessee, 1909).

C. B.

Easter, 1910.

PREFACE

THERE is no plant in the spiritual garden
of the Church of England which at the
present moment needs more diligent
watering and tending than the practical,
devotional study of Holy Scripture. The
extent to which spiritual sloth, or re-
action against Protestant individualism,
or the excuse of critical difficulties is
allowed to minister to the neglect of this
most necessary practice, is greatly to be
deplored. It is surprising in how few
parts of the Bible critical difficulties, be
they what they may, need be any bar
to its practical use.

The present exposition is, I trust, based
upon a careful study of the original text,
but it is, as presented, intended simply
to assist ordinary people to meditate on
the Sermon on the Mount in the Revised
Version, and to apply its teaching to
their own lives. If it proves useful, I
hope, as occasion offers, to follow it up

with other similar expositions of St. Paul's epistles to the Romans and Ephesians, and the epistles of St. John.

My original intention was to publish some lectures given in Westminster Abbey on the Sermon on the Mount in Lent and Easter, 1895. But the attempt to correct for the press a report of those lectures was practically abandoned, and the exposition as now printed is a new one.

It is intended to suggest thoughts rather than to develop them, and to minister to practical reflection rather than to intellectual study ; and I have ventured, in view of this latter aim, to omit almost all references and discussions such as involve footnotes.

I owe as much gratitude as usual to the Rev. Richard Rackham, my brother in the Community of the Resurrection, for help in the correction of proofs.

C. G.

RADLEY,
All Saints' Day, 1896.

TABLE OF CONTENTS

ANALYSIS

OF

THE SERMON ON THE MOUNT

THE

SERMON ON THE MOUNT

CHAPTER I

THE SERMON

I

WHAT is the Sermon on the Mount? It is the moral law of the kingdom of Christ, or in other words it occupies in the New Testament the place which in the Old Testament is occupied by the Ten Commandments. It is thus an excellent example of the relation of the two divine "testaments," or rather covenants, to one another. There is a sentence of St. Augustine's on this subject which it would be useful for every one to have constantly in mind. "We do wrong," he says, "to the Old Testament if we deny that it comes from the same just and good God as the New. On the other hand, we do wrong to the New Testament if we put the Old on a level with it." [1] This is a general statement of the relation between the two covenants, and it applies especially to the moral law. The moral law of the Old Testament, as it is expressed in the Ten Commandments, was the utterance of the same God who now speaks to us in the person of Jesus Christ. It reappears here in the Sermon on the Mount, but deepened and developed. We may say with truth that the Sermon on the Mount supersedes the Ten Commandments ; but it supersedes them by including them in a greater, deeper, and more positive whole.

This Sermon on the Mount, then, is the moral law of the new kingdom, the kingdom of heaven, the kingdom of the Messiah. We have been used to think of the Messiah, the Christ, as an isolated figure ; but the Messiah whose advent is expected in the Old Testament is only the centre of the Messianic kingdom. Round about the king is the kingdom. The king implies the kingdom as the kingdom implies the king. Thus the way

[1] *De Gest. Pelag.* v. (15).

in which Christ announced His Messiah-
ship was by the phrase " The kingdom
of heaven is at hand." And now—now
that He has gathered round Him his
first disciples—He takes them apart, and
there on the mountain He announces to
them the moral law of the new kingdom
to which they are to belong. Thus it is
a law not only for individual consciences,
but for a society—a law which, recognized
and accepted by the individual conscience,
is to be applied in order to establish a
new social order. It is the law of a
kingdom, and a kingdom is a graduated
society of human beings in common subordination to their king.

But observe, what we have here is
law—law, not grace. In St. Paul's phrase,
it is letter, not spirit. When St. Paul
says that " the letter killeth, but the
spirit giveth life," [1] he means this—that
an external written commandment (that
is, the letter) is capable of informing
our consciences, of telling us what God's
will is, of bowing us down to the dust
with a sense of our inability to fulfil it ;
but it is not capable of going further.
Thus it " killeth " ; it makes us conscious

[1] 2 Cor. iii. 6.

of our sin, of our powerlessness, but it
leaves it for something else to put life
into us to do the thing we ought. That
life-giving power is the Spirit. Thus the
law, by informing, kills us : the Spirit,
by empowering, gives us life. Observe,
it is a good, a necessary thing to be thus
killed. The perilous state is "to be
alive without the law," [1] that is, to have
an unenlightened conscience and be living
in a false peace. "If the light that is
in thee be darkness, how great is that
darkness." The first thing is to know
what we ought to do ; and the very fact
that we feel our powerlessness to do it,
makes us ready to offer the cry, the
appeal for divine help.

Again I would ask you to notice a
sentence of Augustine's, which is full of
meaning : "The law was given that
men might seek grace ; grace was given
that the law might be fulfilled." [2]

Thus what we have here, in the Sermon
on the Mount, is the climax of law, the
completeness of the letter, the letter
which killeth ; and because it is so much
more searching and thorough than the
Ten Commandments, therefore does it

[1] Rom. vii. 9.   [2] *De Sp. et Lit.* 34.

kill all the more effectually. It makes
us all the more conscious of sin ; all the
more full of the clamorous demand that
God, who asks such things of us, shall
give us also the power to fulfil them.
But just as in many departments of
human life " man's necessity is God's
opportunity," just as in some well-con-
structed drama the very culminating
moment of difficulty suggests the immediate arrival of release, so it is here. The
divine requirement is pressed home with
unequalled force upon the conscience,
but it is pressed home not in the form of
mere laws of conduct, but (as we shall
see) as a type of character,—not out of
the thick darkness by an inaccessible
God, but by the Divine Love manifested
in manhood and pledging His own faith-
fulness that he who hungers shall be
satisfied and he who asks shall be heard.
The hard demand of the letter is here
in the closest possible connexion with
the promise of the Spirit.

II

You will often see it noticed that a
resemblance to some of the precepts in
the Sermon on the Mount is to be dis-

covered, not only in the Old Testament, on which the whole is confessedly based, but in the sayings of Jewish fathers, or in heathen philosophers and writers, like Confucius among the Chinese, and Socrates or Plato among the Greeks; and this has at times distressed Christians jealous of the unique glory of their religion.   Thus they have sometimes sought to account for the coincidences between " inspired " and " uninspired " authors, or between the divine and the human speakers, by supposing that even heathen writers borrowed from the Old Testament.   They were forgetting surely a great truth, a truth of which in the early centuries the minds of men were full :   that Christ is the Word ;   and it is through fellowship in the Word, who is also the Reason of God, that all men are   rational.   Christ,   therefore,   is   the light   which   in   conscience   and   reason lightens every man from end to end of history.   Christ has been at work, moving by His Spirit in the consciousness of man, so that the whole moral develop-ment of mankind, the whole moral educa-tion of the human race, is of one piece from end to end.   There moves in it

the same Spirit, there expresses itself
the same Word. So that, as we should
expect, there are fragments of the moral
truth which in the Sermon on the Mount
is completely delivered, fragments—
greater or smaller, we need not now
discuss—to be found among the Chinese,
the Japanese, the Greeks, the Indians,
because God left Himself nowhere without witness, the witness of His Word
and Spirit in the hearts of men.[1]

But what we also find to be true is,
that the moral law here given supersedes
the moral law as it is found among
heathen nations or even among the Jews,
by including it in a greater whole. We
may compare the morality of this Sermon
with that expressed by other religious
teachers in several ways.

1. The Sermon on the Mount compared
with the summaries of moral duty belonging to other religions is comprehensive
while they are fragmentary. No moral
code can be produced which approaches
this in completeness or depth. There is
no other moral code belonging to an
accepted and ancient religion for which

[1] See especially St. John i. 4–12, Rom. ii. 14–16,
Acts xvii. 22–31.

any educated European could even claim finality and completeness. We know what John Stuart Mill, though not a believer, said about our Lord's moral teaching. He said " Not even now would it be easy, even for an unbeliever, to find a better translation of the rule of virtue from the abstract into the concrete, than to endeavour so to live that Jesus Christ would approve our life." And Dr. Pusey commented on that by saying " If men would set this before themselves, there would be fewer unbelievers.' [1] There is then, I say, no other moral summary belonging to an ancient religion on behalf of which a man of modern enlightenment could, with a reasonable chance of being listened to, make the claim that its principles can never be outgrown or found insufficient for any race of men. This is to others as the comprehensive to the fragmentary.

2. It is as the pure to the partially corrupt or mixed. Origen, in commenting on the words of the twelfth Psalm, " the words of the Lord are pure words, even

[1] Mill's *Three Essays on Theism*, p. 255. Pusey's *Univ. Sermons*, 1864–72, " God and human independence," p. 10, note 1.

as the silver which from the earth is
tried and purified seven times in the
fire," contrasts in this respect the sacred
writings of the heathen with those of
the Christians. "For though there are
noble words among those who are not
Christians, yet they are not *pure*, because
they are mixed up with so much that is
false." Take for an example the Sym-
posium of Plato. You find in it much
that is most noble about divine love;
but you find this noble element mixed
with dross, that is with acquiescence in
some of the foulest practices of Greek
life. The same is true of the sacred
books of Buddhism. The Sermon on
the Mount, then, is to other moral codes
as the pure to the mixed or partially
corrupt.

3. It is as teaching for grown men,
who are also free, compared to teaching
for children and slaves. It teaches, not
by negative enactments or by literal
enactments at all, but by principles,
positive and weighty principles, embodied
in proverbs which must be apprehended
in their inner spirit and reapplied continually anew as circumstances change.

4. Lastly, it differs from other codes

by the authoritative sanction which is given to the words by the person of the speaker. " He spoke as one having authority, and not as the scribes." All the weight of His mysterious person, all the majesty of His tone, His demeanour, His authority, go to give sanction to this law which He uttered : and not only to give it sanction, in the sense of making men feel that they were dealing with one whose mysterious power it would be better not to offend : His person gives sanction to His words also by inspiring the profoundest confidence that He who makes the claim will also provide strength to correspond with it.

III

I must say one word about a problem which could not by any means be satisfactorily dealt with in the space now at our disposal.

We know that the critics of the Gospel narratives are in our time occupied with nothing so much as with the difficult problem of the relation which the Gospels bear to one another. This problem presents itself in connexion with our present subject.

The Sermon on the Mount as given in
St. Matthew corresponds, though with
many differences, to what you find scat-
tered over a great number of different
chapters in St. Luke—vi. 20–49, xi. 1–4,
9–13, 33–36, xii. 22–31, 58–59, xiii. 24–27,
xiv. 34–35, xvi. 13, 17–18.[1] Now what
are we to say about the relation of these
two accounts of the same teaching ?
There is a good deal that is most characteristic in St. Matthew's sermon which
has nothing corresponding to it in the
other evangelist, e.g. the spiritual treatment of the Commandments and of the
typical religious duties of prayer, almsgiving and fasting ; but where they are
on the same ground they are often so
closely similar that it is plain they are
drawing from the same source.   Whether
this source was oral or written is a question
we need not now discuss ; but what are
we to say of the different treatment of
the same material ?

It is throughout the method of St.
Matthew to collect or group similar in-
cidents or sayings. Thus he gives us a
group of miracles (ch. viii–ix), a group of

---

[1] The Sermon with the parallel passages is given at
length in Appendix I., pp. 202 ff.

seven parables (ch. xiii), a long denuncia-
tion of the Pharisees which is represented
in two different passages of St. Luke's
Gospel (ch. xxiii), and a great group of
discourses about " the end " of which
the same thing may be said (ch. xxiv).
Judging from his general method, then,
we should conclude that in the Sermon
on the Mount we have grouped together
sayings which probably were uttered in
fact, as St. Luke represents, on different
occasions. For it is St. Luke's intention
throughout to present events " in order,"
and the sayings of Christ each in its
proper context.

But it must not be forgotten that a
teacher who, like our Lord, teaches by
way of " sentences " or proverbs, is sure
to repeat the same truth in different
forms and from different points of view.
Those who have examined Francis Bacon's
note-books and published works tell us
how those weighty sentences of his were
written down again and again and reappear continually in slightly different
shapes. So we may suppose it probable
that our Lord frequently repeated similar
utterances.

Thus if St. Luke truly represents that

our Lord on a certain occasion consoled
His disciples by short and emphatic
benedictions pronounced on the actual
poverty in which they lived and the
actual persecutions which they endured
—" Blessed are ye poor, blessed are ye
that hunger now, blessed are ye that
weep now, blessed are ye when men hate
you "—it does not by any means follow
that He did not on another occasion
pronounce, as recorded by St. Matthew,
similar benedictions, more numerous, more
general, and more spiritual, beginning
with one not now on certain actually
poor men, but on the " poor in spirit "
in general. Thus on another occasion [1]
He repeated the saying, " How hardly
shall they that have riches enter into
the kingdom of God," in the more spiritual
form, " How hard it is for them that
trust in riches to enter into the kingdom
of God." Again, it does not follow that
because He gave the pattern prayer in
a shorter form, as recorded by St. Luke,
He should not also have given it in the
longer form, as recorded by St. Matthew.

The collection of our Lord's discourses

[1] If the reading, and not the margin, of the R.V. be
right in Mark x. 23, 24.

which characterizes the first Gospel is—
there is every reason to believe—the
work of the apostle St. Matthew. If
so, we need to remember that it was the
work not only of a first-rate witness, but
also of one whose memory, naturally
retentive, was quickened by a special
gift of the divine Spirit bestowed on the
apostles " to bring to their remembrance
all that Christ had said unto them." [1]

[1] St. John xiv. 26.

CHAPTER II

THE BEATITUDES IN GENERAL

" And seeing the multitudes, he went up into the mountain : and when he had sat down, his disciples came unto him : and he opened his mouth and taught them, saying,

Blessed are the poor in spirit : for theirs is the kingdom of heaven.

Blessed are they that mourn : for they shall be comforted.

Blessed are the meek : for they shall inherit the earth.

Blessed are they that hunger and thirst after righteousness : for they shall be filled.

Blessed are the merciful : for they shall obtain mercy.

Blessed are the pure in heart : for they shall see God.

Blessed are the peacemakers : for they shall be called sons of God.

Blessed are they that have been persecuted for righteousness' sake : for theirs is the kingdom of heaven. Blessed are ye when men shall reproach you, and persecute you, and say all manner of evil against you falsely, for my sake. Rejoice, and be exceeding glad : for great is your reward in heaven : for so persecuted they the prophets which were before you."

OUR Lord went up into the mountain to get away from the multitudes. Thither He was followed by His chosen disciples, and it is to them that the Sermon is uttered. It was spoken to the Church, not to the world ; but as ' the multi-

tudes ' appear also to have listened [1] to it,
we may say that it was spoken into the ear
of the Church and overheard by the world.

1. It begins with the familiar " Beatitudes." They are a description of the
character of the citizen of the new kingdom ; that is, the character of the man
who, enjoying the freedom of the kingdom
of God, has entered into the inheritance
of true blessedness. Observe, we have
a description of a certain character, not
of certain acts. Christ requires us not
to do such and such things, but to be
such and such people. And the character
which we find here described is beyond
all question nothing else than our Lord's
own character put into words, the human
character of our Lord corresponding
always in flawless perfection with the
teaching which He gave. Here are two
reasons why our Lord's teaching is capable
of universal and individual application :
(1) because it is not made up of detailed
commandments, but is the description of
a character which, in its principles, can
be apprehended and embodied in all
possible circumstances : (2) because it is
not only a description in words but a

[1] St. Matt. vii. 28.

description set side by side with a living example.

And we cannot remind ourselves too early that this is the character by which we shall be finally judged. It is " by this man," as St. Paul says, " God will judge the world." And St. John says " we shall be like him, for we shall see him as he is." [1] The estimate of our worth in God's sight depends simply on this, How like are we, or rather, how like are we becoming to the character of Christ ? But of this we shall have opportunity of speaking later on.

2. The beatitudes describe the blessed life—in other words, the citizen of the new kingdom is one who can say with Mary " all generations shall call me blessed."

The idea of a blessed life had been common. We cannot begin to think about life without seeing that there are certain conditions which a man's life must have if we are to be able to congratulate him on being alive. What sort of life is worth living ? That is a question thinking men have asked from old days. Gautama and Confucius, Plato and Aristotle asked it. What sort of life possesses

[1] Acts xvii. 31 ; 1 St. John iii. 2–3.

2

the characteristics which make it blessed —what sort of life can you congratulate a man, thoroughly and heartily, upon living?

Now observe a contrast in the answers given. To Gautama, the Buddha, the existence not merely of selfishness, but of the self, is a fundamental evil, delusion, and source of misery; and the true blessedness of painless peace is only to be attained by the emptying out of all desire, the extinction of all clinging to existence, and so at last by the extinction of life or personality itself. Thus though the Buddha's moral teaching has many beautiful resemblances to that of our Lord, it has this fundamental difference, that Buddha regarded personal existence as a delusion and an evil to be got rid of, but Christ as a supreme truth and good to be at last realized in the vision of God and the fruition of eternal life. " I came that they may have life and may have it abundantly."

Again, Aristotle asked the question, What is the blessed life? and he came to the conclusion that the life truly worth living was possible only for very few men. It was impossible for slaves, because they were the mere tools of other men; or

for the diseased, because they were necessarily miserable ; or for paupers, because
they had not a sufficiency of this world's
goods ; or for those dying young, because
they had not time enough to realize
true blessedness. Observe, I say, the
contrast in all this. Christ lays the
blessed life open to all. And why ?
Because he takes a man at once up to
God : He centres his life on God : He
puts him in full view of God as the
goal of life : He bases life on God as a
foundation. Again, as a consequence of
this, He calculates life—as a life lived in
God must be calculated—on the scale
of eternity. Grant these two things—
that each human life may be based on
God and calculated on the scale of eternity
—and you get rid of all the limitations
which made Aristotle declare that neither
the slave, nor the diseased, nor the poor,
nor those who die young, can live the
blessed life. Thus our Lord has described
the character of true blessedness as belonging to man as man, to all men if
they will have it, simply by the recognition of their true relation to God.
From that point of view all accidents of
life fade away into insignificance. They

give, indeed, its special character to each life, and the conditions of its probation, but they cannot touch its true blessedness.

We can go one step farther. If you take the latter parts of the beatitudes, you will find in them a more detailed account of the blessed life. The end of each beatitude tells us what our Lord meant by blessedness. "Theirs is the kingdom of heaven; they shall be comforted; they shall inherit the earth; they shall be filled; they shall obtain mercy; they shall see God; they shall be called sons of God." All the last six of these seven expressions may be said simply to expand the first. They amplify the idea of membership in the kingdom of heaven. Membership in the kingdom is a life of perfect relationship with man and nature based on perfect fellowship with God. That is true blessedness, and that is open to all. Therein is consolation after all troubles; there is the freedom to move about with a sense of heirship in God's world, as in our legitimate heritage and with no fear of being turned out; there is the satisfaction of all legitimate aspiration; there is gracious acceptance at all hands; there is the

vision of all truth and beauty and goodness, in God; there is final and full
recognition. That is true blessedness.
That is the life which our Lord promises
to every one who will simply put himself
in the right relation to God.

3. There is only one more point that
we need notice with regard to these
beatitudes as a whole, and it concerns
their order. Our Lord begins with strong
paradoxes: Blessed are the poor—the
mourners—the meek. That is to say in
other words, He first describes the true
character by its contrast to the character
of the world. We frequently have occasion to use the expression "the world."
Let me, therefore, once for all explain
what I understand by it when it is used
in a bad sense. It means, of course,
not God's creation as such, which was
pronounced very good. When "the
world" is spoken of in a bad sense—
the worldly world—you may define it
in this way: it is human society or-
ganizing itself apart from God. That
is what in the Bible is meant by "the
world." Well, the world notoriously
clutches at all the gold it can get. The
world avoids all the pain and suffering

it possibly can, avoids it with a calcula-
ting selfishness. The world shrinks from
nothing so much as from humiliation,
and says " Assert yourself and your rights
as much as you can." Our Lord then
describes the true blessedness, first of all
negatively in the first three beatitudes
by strong and marked contrasts to the
character of the world : blessed are the
poor, blessed are the meek, blessed are
the mourners. Then He goes on to give
its positive characteristics : its strong
spiritual appetite for righteousness ; its
active and vigorous compassionateness ;
its single-mindedness or purity of heart ;
the deliberate aim it has to promote the
kingdom of peace. Then, in the last
beatitude, He answers the question how
is such a character likely to find itself
in such a world ; and answers that
question in terms very like those employed
by a Jewish writer, possibly not very
long before our Lord's time, the writer
of the Book of Wisdom, who describes
the attitude of the world towards the
righteous thus :

" But let us lie in wait for the righteous man,
    Because he is of disservice to us
    And is contrary to our works,

And upbraideth us with sins against the law,
And layeth to our charge sins against our discipline.
He professeth to have knowledge of God,
And nameth himself servant of the Lord.
He became to us a reproof of our thoughts.
He is grievous unto us even to behold,
Because his life is unlike other men's,
And his paths are of strange fashion.
We were accounted of him as base metal,
And he abstaineth from our ways as from unclean-
    nesses.
The latter end of the righteous he calleth happy;
And he vaunteth that God is his father.
Let us see if his words be true,
And let us try what shall befall in the ending of
    his life.
For if the righteous man is God's son, he will
    uphold him,
And he will deliver him out of the hand of his
    adversaries.
With outrage and torture let us put him to the test,
That we may learn his gentleness,
And may prove his patience under wrong.
Let us condemn him to a shameful death;
For he shall be visited according to his words.

Thus reasoned they, and they were led astray;
For their wickedness blinded them,
And they knew not the mysteries of God,
Neither hoped they for wages of holiness,
Nor did they judge that there is a prize for blameless
    souls." [1]

    .   .   .   .   .

"Blessed are ye when men shall reproach you,
and persecute you, and say all manner of evil against
you falsely, for my sake. Rejoice, and be exceeding
glad: for great is your reward in heaven: for so
persecuted they the prophets which were before you."

[1] Wisdom ii. 12 ff.

CHAPTER III

THE BEATITUDES IN DETAIL

I

"Blessed are the poor in spirit: for theirs is the kingdom of heaven."

THE Old Testament is full of descriptions of the spirit of the world, the spirit of selfish wealth with its attendant cruelty : and by contrast to this are descriptions of the oppressed poor who are the friends of God. Our Lord took up all this language upon His own lips when, as St. Luke records, He turned to His disciples and said " Blessed are ye poor . . . woe unto you that are rich." But all the actually poor are not the disciples of Christ. It is possible to combine the selfishness and grasping avarice of " the rich " with the condition of poverty. So our Lord has, as recorded by St. Matthew, gone beneath the surface and based His kingdom, the character of His citizens, not upon actual poverty, but

24

upon detachment.   The world says " Get all you can, and keep it."   Christ says, Blessed are those who at least in heart and will have nothing.

There is one verse in the Old Testament which describes this poverty of spirit.   It is the utterance of Job : [1]   " The Lord gave, and the Lord hath taken away ; blessed be the name of the Lord."   There is pure, perfect detachment.   Job took and used aright what God gave him, adoring the sovereignty of God.   The sovereign took away what He had given ; Job gave it up freely.   Being detached— that is poverty of spirit ; at the least, " having food and covering, let us be therewith content." [2]

Our Lord says then, Blessed are those who are thus detached ; and of course we look to Him for illustration, for these beatitudes express His own character.   He was detached.   The Incarnation was a self-emptying.   He clung not to all the glories of heaven, but " emptied Himself " and " beggared Himself," as St. Paul says.[3]   Then when He had been born a man, He set the example of clinging to nothing external.   He aban-

[1] Job i. 21.   [2] 1 Tim. vi. 8.   [3] Phil. ii. 7, 2 Cor. viii. 9.

2*

doned ease, popularity, the favour of the great, even the sympathy of His friends, even, last and greatest of all, on the cross, the consolation of the divine presence. Each privilege in turn was abandoned without a murmur, not, speaking generally, on the ascetic principle, but because moral obedience to God in fulfilment of His mission required it. He became utterly naked, poorer than the poorest ; therefore in a supreme sense " His was the kingdom of heaven." He stood empty, persecuted, before Pilate, and said " Thou sayest that I am a king "; and the moral conscience of the world has witnessed that He spoke truth. So we, like Him, are to be ready to surrender, ready to give up ; and in proportion to this detachment, in proportion as we do really in will adore the sovereignty of God, and are ready to receive and to give up according to His will, in that proportion are all the hindrances removed by which the royalty of His kingdom is prevented from entering into our hearts and lives. St. Paul's comment on this first beatitude lies in his description of the apostles " As having nothing, and yet possessing all things " ; or in his encouragement to Christians generally " All things are yours." [1] The wilfulness with which we cling to supposed " necessaries of life," " things we cannot do without " ; false claims on life for enjoyments which we should be the stronger for dispensing with ; false ideals of vanity and display— these, and not our circumstances, are the hindrances to that largeness of heart and peace and liberty and joy, which have their root only in the bare and naked relation of the soul to God.

The splendid promise attached to this beatitude brings it into contrast with an old Jewish saying which has many parallels, " Ever be more and more lowly in spirit, for the prospect of man is to become the food of worms." The motive to humility which our Lord suggests is very different.

Before we pass on, let us observe how important it is that there should be at all times those in the Church who are capable, not merely of poverty in spirit, but voluntarily of poverty in fact. Upon all men our Lord enjoins detachment. But upon one young man in particular He enjoined that he should give his

[1] 2 Cor. vi. 10, 1 Cor. iii. 21.

possessions away, that he should sell all
that he had and give to the poor. So in
the Church there have been those who in
the religious orders have dedicated themselves in voluntary poverty to the service
of God and of man ; and the Church
has lost incalculably in ages when there
have been none such. Like all other
institutions, the religious orders have
been liable to great abuses : they have
been homes very often, not so much of
scandalous vices, as of sloth and corporate
greed ; but we must not give up the
ideal because there are abuses. There is
the command of the Lord to all to be,
like Job, detached ; there is the counsel
of the Lord to some to be, in fact, voluntarily poor.

II

"Blessed are they that mourn : for they shall be
comforted."

These beatitudes follow one another,
as St. Chrysostom says, in a golden
chain. Once again our Lord is putting
Himself in startling opposition to one of
the favourite maxims of the world. The
world says " Get as much pleasure as you
can out of life ; suck it in wherever

you can; and hug yourself as close as you can from all that disquiets you or makes you uncomfortable; in a word, get as much pleasure and avoid as much pain as by intelligence and forethought you can possibly do." In startling opposition to this maxim of the world our Lord puts His maxim " Blessed are they that mourn."

What does that mean ? Briefly : there are two chief kinds of mourning into which it is the duty of every true servant of our Lord to enter—the mourning for sin and the mourning for pain. We must mourn for sin, for we are sinners. It is possible to hide the fact from our eyes, to prevent the inconvenient light from coming in upon our consciences, to suppose that things that are widely tolerated must be tolerable, that things that are frequently or habitually done must have something to say for themselves. But the Christian gets into the light ; he lets the light of the divine word go down into his heart ; he strives to see himself first, in the silence of his own soul, as the Lord sees him. Thus he is brought to repentance, and repentance which is in regard to the future a " change of purpose," is with respect to the past a true mourning : if not emotional sorrow, still profound and heartfelt regret on account of those things in which we have gone against the will of God : and " blessed are they that mourn."

Next to this mourning for sin is the mourning of sympathy with others' pain. There are moments when a Christian may legitimately, like his Lord in the garden of Gethsemane, be engrossed in the bearing of " his own burden." [1] But in the main a Christian ought, like his Lord, or like St. Paul, to have his own burden so well in hand, that he is able to leave the large spaces of his heart for other people to lay their sorrows upon. " Bear ye one another's burdens." [2] Of our Lord it was said " Himself took our infirmities, and bare our diseases " [3]— not on the cross simply, but as He moved about in Galilee and Judæa, and the sad, the sorrowful and the sick came to Him. It is always possible to use the advantages of a comparatively prosperous position to exempt ourselves, to screen ourselves off, from the common lot of pain. This is to shut ourselves off from

[1] Gal. vi. 5.   [2] Gal. vi. 2.   [3] St. Matt. viii. 17.

true fruitfulness and final joy. " Except a grain of wheat fall into the earth and die, it abideth by itself alone ; but if it die, it beareth much fruit. He that loveth his life, loseth it ; and he that hateth his life in this world shall keep it unto life eternal." [1] " Blessed are they that mourn."

" He that lacks time to mourn, lacks time to mend.
  Eternity mourns that. 'Tis an ill cure
  For life's worst ills, to have no time to feel them.
  Where sorrow's held intrusive and turn'd out
  There wisdom will not enter, nor true power,
  Nor aught that dignifies humanity."

And in proportion to the fullness with which you enter into penitence for sin and into sympathy for the sufferings of men, you shall get, not the miserable laughter of forgetfulness, which lasts but for a moment, but the comfort (or encouragement) of God. " That we may be able to comfort them that are in any affliction, through the comfort wherewith we ourselves are comforted of God." [2] " The sorrow of the world worketh death," but " godly sorrow worketh repentance unto salvation, not to be repented of.[3] "

[1] St. John xii. 24, 25.   [2] 2 Cor. i. 4.
[3] 2 Cor. vii. 10.

" Blessed are they that mourn : for they shall be comforted."

And here, by way of warning, let me point out that there is a false as well as a true mourning. It is possible to be discontented with the world but to lack the courage of faith which makes our discontent fruitful of reform. It is possible to be discontented with ourselves, and yet never so simply and humbly make our confession to God our Father as to get the joy which comes of being forgiven. We are discontented ; but our discontent is pride, not the humility of true sorrow. It will not be comforted, it will not thankfully take the divine offer of absolution. The " woman that was a sinner " made no delay in believing herself forgiven, but set to work at once to show the love which springs of gratitude in the heart of those who accept their release. The false sorrow of pride was noticed by one of the leaders of monasticism in the west—Cassian, who describes and contrasts thus the true sorrow and the false : [1]

" But that sorrow which ' worketh repentance unto stable salvation ' is

[1] *Institutes*, ix. 11.

obedient, approachable, humble, amiable, gentle and patient, inasmuch as it comes down from the love of God and, inspired with the desire of perfection, gives itself over unweariedly to all pain of body and contrition of spirit ; and having a happiness of its own and a vitality which comes from the hope of progress, it keeps all the amiability of an approachable and patient disposition, possessing in itself all the fruits of the Holy Spirit which the apostle enumerates. But the false sorrow is bitter, impatient, hard, full of rancour and fruitless grief, and penal despair, breaking off and recalling the man whom it has got into its grasp from industry and salutary sorrow, because it is irrational, and not only impedes the efficacy of prayers but also empties out of the soul all those spiritual fruits which the true sorrow knows how to impart."

III

"Blessed are the meek : for they shall inherit the earth."

Still our Lord is explaining the character of the kingdom by contrast to the ideals of the world. The world says "Stand up for your rights ; make the most of yourself ; don't let any man put upon you." And so we are always standing on our dignity, always thinking ourselves insulted or imposed upon. " Blessed are the meek," our Lord says. The meek —that is manifestly, those who are ready to be put upon as far as they themselves are concerned. This is the character of our Lord, who, " when he was reviled, reviled not again ; when he suffered, threatened not ; but committed himself to him that judgeth righteously." [1]

Of course, from another point of view, we may be quite bound from time to time to assert ourselves. Our Lord recognizes that, as we shall have an opportunity of noticing in another connexion. We may have to assert ourselves for the sake of the moral order of the church and of the world. But no one gets true peace, or has really got to the foundation of things, until, as far as his own dignity is concerned, he is in a position to say, You can wrong God and you can wrong society ; and it may be my duty to stand up for God and for society ; but me, as far as I am concerned, you cannot provoke. That is the ideal to which we have to

[1] 1 Peter ii. 23.

attain. That is the meekness which is appropriate to sinners like ourselves who know what we deserve, who *on a general review of life* can seldom feel that we are suffering unmerited wrong ; but it is the meekness also of the sinless and righteous one.

And the result of this entire absence of self-assertion is that we can make no claim on the world which God will not at the last substantiate. " Blessed are the meek "—our Lord is here quoting the psalm—" for they shall *inherit* the earth." [1] What is an heir ? An heir is a person who enters into rightful pos- session. He is in no fear that any other can ever come and turn him out. He moves at ease amongst his possessions, because the things that he inherits are really his. No one with a better claim can come to oust him. Now, if we go about the world making claims on society which God does not authorize, refusing to bear what God will have us bear, the day will come when the true Master appears, and we shall be exposed to shame. We have made claims which He did not authorize ; we have asserted our-

[1] Ps. xxxvii. 29.

selves where He gave us no right or title
to assert ourselves ; we shall be ousted.
But the meek, who ever committed themselves to Him that judgeth righteously,
have nothing to fear. " Friend, come up
higher," is all that is before them. They
will simply, in steady and royal advance,
enter into the full heritage of that which
men kept back from them, but God has
in store for them.

IV

"Blessed are they that hunger and thirst after
righteousness : for they shall be filled."

In strong, bold outlines our Lord has
begun by sketching for us the character
of His citizens in marked contrast to the
ideals of the world. But He is not
satisfied with giving us these, as it were,
negative characteristics ; He passes on
to more positive traits. The citizens of
the new kingdom " hunger and thirst after
righteousness." Every one knows what
appetite is, what hunger and thirst mean.
It is a strong craving, a craving which
must be satisfied, or we perish. You
cannot forget that you are hungry or
thirsty. And in human pursuits we again
and again see what is like hunger and

thirst. You see an appetite for place;
a man is bent upon it; he will by whatever means get that position which his
soul desires. So again you see in men's
amusements a similar craving. Go to
the side of the Thames at Putney, and
you may see two crews of eight men
practising there for a famous race, their
supporters and backers looking on. All
is eagerness, and there is not the slightest
betrayal of consciousness that anything
in the world could be more important
than the winning of that race. That is
what may be truly called a hunger and
thirst. And such is the appetite for
righteousness which possesses the citizens
of our Lord's kingdom. Righteousness,
or rather *the* righteousness, that character
which God has marked out for us, the
character of Christ—blessed are they
which do hunger and thirst after it.

Brethren, we so often feel hopeless
about getting over our faults. Let us
hunger and thirst after righteousness,
and we shall be filled. As our Lord saw
of the travail of His soul and was satisfied,
so, depend upon it, shall we. If you
only seriously want to be good, your
progress may be slow, but at the last you

will be good.   Christ is pledged to satisfy,
if only you will go on wanting.   There
is not in the pursuit of goodness any
failure except in ceasing to hunger and
thirst—that is, in ceasing to want, to pray,
to try.   Do you want righteousness seriously, deliberately ?   Then you can have
it, and not for yourself only, but for the
world.   " Till righteousness turn again
unto judgement, all such as are true in
heart shall follow it."   It is pledged to
us.   The day will come when the kingdom
of heaven, the kingdom of righteousness
and meekness and truth, shall be an
established and a visible fact.   Blessed
are they that here and now hunger and
thirst after righteousness in themselves
and in the world :   for they shall be
filled.

V

"Blessed are the merciful : for they shall obtain mercy."

Of course wherever human misery is,
there is also human pity.   But, apart
from Christ, it was not thought of as a
motive force, to be used in redeeming
others' lives and in enriching our own.
The Buddha, indeed, one of the purest
and noblest men who have ever lived, was

first awakened from the dream of luxury, in which he had been brought up, by the threefold spectacle of human misery— decrepitude, disease and death.   And once awakened, he made his " great renuncia- tion " :   he abandoned his royal state : after much searching, he discovered for himself, as he thought, the way of eman- cipation from life and, being filled with compassion, taught it to others.   But he believed life to be radically an evil.   He could imagine no redemption *of* life but only escape *from* it.   The philosopher Aristotle, who examined and catalogued human qualities, could not have failed to come across the fact of pity.   But he seems even to have regarded it as a troublesome emotion—a disturbing force which had better be got rid of in practical concerns.   The Greek tragedy, which by its marvellous presentations of the weak- ness of man was calculated to evoke the sentiment of pity in great intensity, he regarded as a vent or outlet for the emotion which in this way could be purged off and leave the Greek citizen in untroubled serenity in face of actual life.   It is to be feared that we very often use the drama and literature in this way.   We let our emotion of pity be stirred by the pictures of human misfortune presented to us, and we find a luxury in the indulgence of the emotion. But it is a luxury, and nothing more. It leads to no effective action for the removing of the misery which we deplore. This is pagan. For the disciple of Christ pity is a motive to vigorous action. God in Christ declares His " power most chiefly in showing mercy and pity." Powerful pity is pity which passes from emotion into practical and redemptive action. Of such pity only does Christ say " Blessed are the merciful or pitiful." Compassion which does nothing is in the New Testament [1] regarded as a form of pernicious hypocrisy.

And the merciful shall obtain mercy. Here we get a great law of the divine dealing. God deals with us as we deal with our fellow-men. In the Old Testament [2] it is said " With the merciful thou, God, wilt show thyself merciful ; with the perfect man thou wilt show thyself perfect ; with the pure thou wilt show thyself pure ; and with the perverse thou wilt show thyself froward." And again,

[1] St. James ii. 15–16 ; 1 John iii. 16–18.
[2] Ps. xviii. 24–26.

in our Lord's parable,[1] when the servant
who had been let off his debts by his
master was found to deal unmercifully
with his fellow-servant who was indebted
to him, the remission was cancelled, and
the weight of his old debt fell back upon
him, to teach us that God deals with us
as we deal with our fellow-men.   Thus
again, in view of the last great day, our
Lord says " Inasmuch as ye did it unto
the least of these my brethren, come ye
blessed, inherit the kingdom."   So in our
Lord's Prayer, we pray " Forgive us our
trespasses, as we forgive them that trespass
against us."   Do we want to know how
our Lord will regard us at the last day ?
We can find the answer by considering
how our face looks, not in mere passing
emotion, but in its serious and deliberate
aspect, towards our fellow-men.   God
deals with us then, as we deal with our
fellows.   Nor need we confine the principle to God's dealings with us.   The
same law is observable in the treatment
we receive at men's hands.   On the
whole we can determine men's attitude to
us by our attitude to them.   Almost all
men have their best selves drawn out

[1] St. Matt. xviii. 23 f.

towards a really compassionate life. " Perchance for a *good* man—one who is not only just, but good—some would even dare to die." [1] " Blessed are the merciful, for they shall obtain mercy."

VI

" Blessed are the pure in heart : for they shall see God."

If we take part in the kingdom, there must be singleness of purpose. Purity of heart is, of course, continually taken in its narrower meaning of absence of sensual defilement and pollution. That is an important part of purity ; and may I say a word about the pursuit of purity in this narrower sense ? A great many people are distressed by impure temptations, and they very frequently fail to make progress with them for one reason, namely, that while they are anxious to get rid of sin in this one respect, they are not trying after goodness as a whole. Uncleanness of life and heart they dislike. It weighs upon their conscience and destroys their self-respect. But they have no similar horror of pride, or irreverence, or uncharity. People very often say

[1] Rom. v. 7.

that it is impossible to lead a " pure " life. The Christian minister is not pledged to deny this, if a man will not try to be religious all round, to be Christ-like altogether. For the way to get over uncleanness is, in innumerable cases, not to fight against that only, but to contend for positive holiness all round, for Christlikeness, for purity of heart in the sense in which Christ used the expression, in the sense in which in the 51st Psalm a clean heart is coupled with a " right spirit "—that is, a will set straight towards God, or simplicity of purpose. There is an old Latin proverb—" Unless the vessel is clean, whatever you pour into it turns sour." It is so with the human will. Unless the human will is directed straight for God, whatever you put into the life of religious and moral effort has a root of bitterness and sourness in it which spoils the whole life. Our Lord means " Blessed are the single-minded," for they, though as yet they may be far from seeing God, though as yet they may not believe a single article of the Christian Creed, yet at last shall attain the perfect vision ; yes, as surely as God is true, they shall be satisfied in their every capacity for truth and beauty and goodness ; they shall behold God.

Any measure of true spiritual illumination, like that of Job when the Lord had answered his questionings, may be described as " seeing God ; " and in this sense to see God is a necessary preliminary to repentance [1] and is requisite for spiritual endurance.[2] But in its full sense it is incompatible with any remaining dissatisfaction ; it is the final goal of human efforts, the reward of those who here are content to " walk by faith, not by sight," and it includes in perfection—what in a measure all discovery after search includes—satisfaction for the intellect, and full attainment for the will, and the ecstasy of the heart, in God as He is.

VII

" Blessed are the peacemakers : for they shall be called sons of God."

Christ is the Prince of Peace. He brings about peace among men, breaking down all middle walls of partition between classes and races and individuals, by

[1] Job xlii. 5, St. Luke v. 8 ; and cf. the vision which is the beginning of purification after death in Cardinal Newman's *Dream of Gerontius.*

[2] Hebr. xi. 27.

making them first of all at peace with God—atonement among men by way of atonement with God. This is the only secure basis of peace. There are many kinds of false and superficial peace, which the Prince of Peace only comes to break up. " I came not to send peace on earth, but a sword." [1] Peace can never be purchased in God's way by the sacrifice of truth. But peace in the truth we, like our Master, must be for ever pursuing.

Do we habitually remember how it offends our Lord to see divisions in the Christian Church, nations nominally Christian armed to the teeth against one another, class against class and individual against individual in fierce and relentless competition, jealousies among clergy and church-workers, communicants who forget that the sacrament of union with Christ is the sacrament of union also with their fellow-men ?

Christians are to be makers of Christ's peace. Something we can all do to reconcile individuals, families, classes, churches, nations. The question is, Are we, as churchmen and citizens, by work and by prayer, in our private conduct

[1] St. Matt. x. 34.

and our public action, doing our utmost
with deliberate, calculated, unsparing
effort ? If so our benediction is the
highest: it is to be, and to be acknowledged as being, sons of God.

VIII

"Blessed are they that have been persecuted for
righteousness' sake: for theirs is the kingdom of
heaven."

There has now been given the picture
of the Christian character in its wonderful attractiveness—that detachment,
that readiness to enter into the heritage of
human pain, that self-suppressing meekness and humility towards our fellow-men,
that strong passion for righteousness, that
effective compassion, that singleness of
heart, that striving for peace. Yet, where
it is not welcomed, it stings by its very
beauty, it hardens by its very holiness.
Thus there came about the strange result,
that when that character was set in its
perfection before men's eyes in the person of our Lord, they would not have
it. They set upon Him and slew Him.
It is in full view of this consequence
of being righteous that our Lord speaks
this last beatitude: and He gives it

pointed and particular application to His disciples.

" Blessed are ye when men shall reproach you, and persecute you, and say all manner of evil against you falsely, for my sake. Rejoice, and be exceeding glad : for great is your reward in heaven : for so persecuted they the prophets which were before you."

THE PLACE OF THE CHRISTIAN CHARACTER IN THE WORLD.

As soon as ever a man sets himself seriously to aim at this Christian character, the devil at once puts this thought into his mind—Am I not aiming at what is too high to be practicable ? am I not aiming too high to do any good ? If I am to help men, surely I must be like them ? I must not be so unworldly, if I am to help men in this sort of world. Now our Lord at once anticipates this kind of argument. He says at once, as it were, No, you are to help men by being unlike them. You are to help men, not by offering them a character which they shall feel to be a little more respectable than their own, but by offering them a character filled with the love of God. They may mock

it for a while; but in the " day of visitation," in the day when trouble comes,
in the day when they are thrown back
on what lies behind respectability, in the
day when first principles emerge, they
will glorify God for the example you
have given them. They will turn to
you then, because they will feel that
you have something to show them that
will really hold water, something that
is really and eternally worth having.

Thus our Lord at once proceeds to
answer the question, How is a character
such as the beatitudes describe, planted
in a world such as this is, to effect good ?
It is to purify by its own distinctive
savour, it is to be conspicuous by its
own splendid truth to its ideal, it is to
arrest attention by its powerful contrast
to the world about it. This is the meaning of the metaphors which follow the
beatitudes :

" Ye are the salt of the earth : but if the salt have
lost its savour, wherewith shall it be salted ? it is
thenceforth good for nothing, but to be cast out
and trodden under foot of men. Ye are the light of
the world. A city set on a hill cannot be hid."

" Ye are the salt of the earth." Salt
is that which keeps things pure by its

emphatic antagonistic savour. " Ye are the light of the world." Light is that which burns distinctively in the darkness. " A city that is set on a hill " is a marked object, arresting attention over a whole country side.

" Ye are the salt of the earth : but if the salt have lost its savour, wherewith shall it be salted ? " The savour of a Christianity which does not mean what it says, wherewith can it be salted ? How can it recover its position and influence ? Would it not be better never to have been Christians at all than to be Christians who do not mean what they say ? What is so useless as a hollow profession of religion ? " It is thence-forth good for nothing, but to be cast out and trodden under foot of men." " I would thou wert cold or hot. So because thou art lukewarm, and neither hot nor cold, I will spew thee out of my mouth." [1] Christians exist in order to make the contrast of their own lives apparent to the world.

[1] Rev. iii. 15–16. These words mean, I think, not " I would that ye, the Church of Laodicea, were either morally worse than ye are or morally better " ; but " I would that either ye were not Christians at all or better Christians."

3

"Neither do men light a lamp, and put it under the bushel, but on the stand ; and it shineth unto all that are in the house. Even so let your light shine before men, that they may see your good works, and glorify your Father which is in heaven."

We may point the significance of this teaching of our Lord by contrasting it with that of another great religious teacher. We have often heard it said that more people are good Mohammedans in Mohammedan countries than good Christians in Christian countries. That may be true, and for this reason : Mohammed set before his disciples an ideal of conduct calculated to commend itself naturally to the people he had to do with. Supposing no fundamental change of character, no real transformation, was required of them, he saw that they would be ready enough to observe religious ceremonies, and to fight, and to abstain from drink. He fastened on these things. These, he said, are what God requires of you. And he has won a high measure of success on the average. Mohammedans have been conspicuous for courage and temperance and regularity in the transaction of religious forms. But just because Mohammed was so easily satisfied,

his religion has been a religion of stagna-
tion. He neither aimed at nor effected
any regeneration of man.

But our Lord said " Except a man be
born again,"—i.e. unless so fundamental
a change take place in him, that it can
only be compared to a fresh birth—" he
cannot see the kingdom of God." And
He made it plain that the working out
of this new birth would not be possible
without the sternest self-denial. For this
very reason our Lord's religion has found
fewer *genuine* adherents than Moham-
medanism, but by means of those who
have been genuine adherents it has effected
a profound spiritual renewal even in
society as a whole.

No doubt the Church has often seemed
to forget her Lord's method. There have
been times—as at the baptism of the
Franks—when the Church incorporated
men in masses, allowing the Christian
standard to be lowered almost indefinitely,
in order that a whole race might be
called Christian. So, again, there was
a time when Jesuit casuists said (in
effect), if only we can keep people Catholic,
making their confessions and receiving
absolution, it shall be done at any cost

of accommodation to existing morals. Once more, the Church of England, in order to maintain the ideal of " a national Church," has in result allowed almost all the power of spiritual discipline, which she should have kept in her own hand, to be surrendered to a Parliament which is in the loosest possible relation to Christianity of any kind.

In each of these cases the Church abandoned the method of Christ : she sacrificed reality to numbers, or genuine discipleship to supposed political influence, and as a result in each case the salt lost its savour.

The question remains for us " Where-with can it be salted ? " Is the savour of true Christianity among us so far gone as to be irrecoverable ? We thank-fully answer No. But if we are to make good our denial, we must set to work to let men understand that, as the Church has a creed which she cannot let go, and a ministry and sacraments which are committed to her to exercise and to dispense, so she has a moral standard, which, if she is not to fall under the curse of barrenness, she must re-erect and be true to. Only when men have come to understand what the Christian moral standard is—in marriage and in the home, in commerce and in politics—and to understand that it can no more be dispensed with than the creed or the sacraments, is there any prospect of a healthy revival of church life.

CHAPTER IV

THE REVISION OF THE OLD LAW

THE character of the citizens of the new kingdom as described by our Lord was so surprising, so paradoxical, that it was inevitable the question should arise, Was He a revolutionary who had come to upset and destroy all the old law—was this a revolutionary movement in the moral and religious world? To this question, then, our Lord directly addressed Himself. The rest of the first chapter of the Sermon on the Mount—St. Matthew v. 17 to the end—is simply a statement of the relation in which this new righteousness, this righteousness of the new kingdom, stands to the old righteousness of the Mosaic Law.

Our Lord explains that the new law stands in a double relation to the old. First, it is in direct continuity with what had gone before (vv. 17–19); and, secondly (vv. 20–48), it supersedes it, as the complete supersedes the incomplete.

(1) The continuity is thus stated :

" Think not that I came to destroy the law or the prophets : I came not to destroy, but to fulfil. For verily I say unto you, Till heaven and earth pass away, one jot or one tittle shall in no wise pass away from the law, till all things be accomplished. Whosoever therefore shall break one of these least commandments, and shall teach men so, he shall be called least in the kingdom of heaven ; but whosoever shall do and teach them, he shall be called great in the kingdom of heaven."

Here we get the divine principle of action. God does not despair of what is imperfect because it is imperfect. He views every institution (or person) not as it is, but as it is becoming ; not by the level of its present attainment, but by the character and direction of its movement. Everything that is moving in the right direction is destined in the divine providence to reach its fulfilment. This was the case pre-eminently with the Old Testament. It was imperfect, but its tendency was directed aright. As St. Irenæus says " The commandments are common to the Jews and us : with them they had their beginning and origin, with us their development and

completion." [1]   And St. Augustine : " The
New Testament is latent in the Old, and
the Old Testament is patent in the New." [2]
Here then we have our chief object-
lesson in the method of divine education.
If we examine the matter in detail, we
shall see that in the New Testament
every element in the Old Testament finds
itself fulfilled.

Is it prophecy, in the sense of pre-
diction ? In the Old Testament an ideal
is projected into the future by inspired
men, and in Christ and His kingdom it
is realized. Moreover, if you look to the
beginning of the Acts of the Apostles
or to St. Matthew's Gospel, you will see
how full the early Christians were of
the sense of this realization, of the sense
that in the Old Testament is a forecast
and in the New a fulfilment. Or is it
the ritual law ? You study its enactments
in Leviticus ; and then you read the
Epistle to the Hebrews. You see how,
to the mind of the spiritual Jewish-
Christian writer, in the old law is external
symbol and in Christ spiritual realization.
Or is it the moral law ? You compare
the Ten Commandments in the Old Testa-

[1] *C. hœr.* iv. 13. 4.   [2] *Quœst.* 73 *in Exod.*

ment with our Lord's Sermon on the Mount or St. James' Epistle. They stand to one another as preliminary education to final enlightenment. And in another sense law altogether is represented by St. Paul as only the training of slaves or children in preparation for the sonship or manhood which is reached when the Spirit is given.

Or, once more, is it types of character that are in question ? You know the old difficulty about Jacob and Esau. How can we approve of Jacob who was so deceitful ? How can we disapprove of Esau who was so generous and impulsive ? The answer is a deep and true one. It is that Esau's impulsive nature led to nothing; he was "profane" ; [1] in fact, Edom—the race of which Esau is the parent and type—produced nothing, changed nothing, brought nothing to perfection. Jacob, for all his mendacity, knew what it was to be in covenant with God, and his race grew into the likeness of God. Israel led to something.

All the imperfect elements in the Old Testament—and, of course, they are imperfect—reach fulfilment in the New.

[1] Hebr. xii. 16.

3*

They enshrine the will of God at a certain stage. Therefore they are worthy of respect. They are to be realized, not violated. And so our Lord goes on to warn His disciples lest, in the enthusiasm of the new teaching, they should think that they could best show their zeal by disparaging elements in the old law under which they had been brought up. For it is always the case that when people have learned something new, their first impulse is to show what they have learned by disparaging what they knew before. Thus our Lord warns them of the low place in His kingdom which they will hold who exhibit towards even the details of the older teaching a spirit of destructiveness, and of the high esteem which will be accorded to the reverent handling of it.

(2) Then our Lord passes to the other side of the question. The old law was imperfect; the new law is to supersede it. The new law is to supersede it both as it is represented in the actual standard of its professors, the scribes and Pharisees (v. 20), and then, more than that, it is to supersede it even in its actual principles (vv. 21–48).

First, as regards its professors :

" For I say unto you, that except your righteousness shall exceed the righteousness of the scribes
and Pharisees, ye shall in no wise enter into the
kingdom of heaven."

It is well known what the scribes and
Pharisees represented. They had left out
of consideration the prophetic teaching
in the Old Testament and the prophetic
element in the books of Moses—all that
made light of outward observances by
contrast with moral holiness or, still
more, as divorced from it. They had
made the observance of the ceremonies
" the be-all and the end-all " of religion.
Thus their religion was pre-eminently
external and, as such, unprogressive. It
was a religion, again, which with the help
of dispensations and evasions could be
practised without much spiritual or moral
effort. Hence it ministered to self-satis-
faction and hypocrisy. Thus our Lord
continually judges it, and here He warns
His disciples not to suppose that His
revision of the old law is to result in the
establishment of an easier religion than
that of scribes and Pharisees. The requirement of obedience will be deeper
and more searching.

But our Lord goes back behind the

professors upon the law itself; and He
proceeds in detail to deal with the old
moral law, in order to deepen it into the
law of His new kingdom.

There are two points to which I would
call attention, which apply to all these
modifications or deepenings of the old
law.

First, notice the authority of the
teacher. " It was said *to* them of old
time "—that is by God Himself in the
Mosaic Law—Thou shalt not do this or
that; " but I say unto you." Now this
is a new tone, and it has only one legitimate explanation. All the prophets had
said " Thus saith the Lord " : they had
spoken the word of another. Jesus says
" I say unto you," thus giving one of
many indications that He who spoke
was different in kind from all other
speakers upon earth; that He was the
fount of the moral law, and could speak
as the one supreme legislator with the
voice, with the authority, of God Himself.

Secondly, notice that when our Lord
deals with the different commandments,
He deals with them on principles which
in each case would apply to all the
others. You could take the distinctive

principle which emerges in His dealing with the law of murder or of adultery, and apply it to the case of all the other commandments.[1] This is only one instance which goes to prove that our Lord does not mean to save us trouble. He teaches in a way which leaves us a great deal to do for ourselves, and requires of us a great deal of moral thoughtfulness.

THE LAW OF MURDER

" Ye have heard that it was said to them of old time, Thou shalt not kill ; and whosoever shall kill shall be in danger of the judgement : but I say unto you, that every one who is angry with his brother shall be in danger of the judgement ; and whosoever shall say to his brother, Raca [vain fellow !], shall be in danger of the council ; and whosoever shall say, Thou fool, shall be in danger of the hell of fire."

In explanation of this let us look at the Second Book of the Chronicles. " And he set judges in the land throughout all the fenced cities of Judah, city by city, and said to the judges, Consider what ye do : for ye judge not for man, but for the Lord ; and he is with you in the judgement. Now therefore let the fear of the Lord be upon you ; take heed and do it : for there is no iniquity with the

[1] This is drawn out in Appendix ii., p. 218.

Lord our God, nor respect of persons, nor taking of gifts. Moreover in Jerusalem did Jehoshaphat set of the Levites and the priests, and of the heads of the fathers' houses of Israel, for the judgement of the Lord, and for controversies." [1]

King Jehoshaphat is here said to have appointed a central court in Jerusalem and local courts in all the towns ; and the arrangement was permanent. The local court or Sanhedrin is apparently what is meant by " the judgement " in this passage of the Sermon, and the central court or supreme Sanhedrin is what is meant by " the council." Now certain even capital offences could be dealt with by the local courts, but the gravest only by the central Sanhedrin. Thus there was a gradation of crimes. Moreover, the Jews believed in an awful penalty after death for those who had egregiously sinned. Gehenna—that is, the Valley of Hinnom, close to Jerusalem—was the place where children had been burnt alive in sacrifice to Moloch ; and it had become later a metaphor for the place of punishment after death. Thus, it appears, the Jews recognized ordinary

---

[1] 2 Chron. xix. 5–8, cf. Josephus *Antiq.* IV. viii. 14.

offences which came before the local
court, special offences which came before the central court, and an awful
penalty after death for the worst sort of
offences.

Now, no offence was brought under the
cognizance of the Jewish law at all which
was not a sin in act; the sin of actual
murder for instance. But our Lord raises
the whole standard of guilt. He takes
no account of sins of act at all. In the
citizens of His new kingdom, sins of act
are, as it were, out of the question. The
way He deals with the law—specifically
the law of murder, but in principle all the
laws—is, if we may paraphrase His words,
this : Under the new law you are to think
of malicious anger, of anger and malice
entertained in your hearts, as under the
old law men were accustomed to think
of ordinary homicide. When this malice
of heart expresses itself in the word of
dislike and contempt, that is a graver
offence, and shall have attached to it the
same moral guilt as would in the old days
have brought a man before the central
court. And the stronger expression of
reprobation, " Thou fool," is a sin which
may bring a man into eternal punish-

ment. " He is liable (literally) up to the point of the Gehenna of fire."

Our Lord certainly speaks in metaphor. Because obviously one could not in fact bring a man under any earthly tribunal for the thoughts of his heart. But the meaning is plain. Our Lord raises deliberately allowed sins of thought and feeling to the level previously occupied by overt acts ; and words He counts yet graver sins ; and the deliberate expression of hatred He counts a sin which may destroy the soul.

This is the way in which He deals with the sixth commandment (though it would apply to all the others). And then He adds a sort of parenthesis dealing with the duty of *hastening* to remove any uncharitable relation in which we may stand towards others.

" If therefore thou art offering thy gift at the altar, and there rememberest that thy brother hath aught against thee, leave there thy gift before the altar, and go thy way, first be reconciled to thy brother, and then come and offer thy gift. Agree with thine adversary quickly, whiles thou art with him in the way ; lest haply the adversary deliver thee to the judge, and the judge deliver thee to the officer, and thou be cast into prison. Verily I say unto thee, Thou shalt by no means come out thence, till thou have paid the last farthing."

Our Lord is speaking to Jews who were accustomed to bring their offerings into the temple. He says that if one of them, while engaged in this religious observance, should remember that his brother has aught against him, he is to leave his gift before the altar and to go away hastily, as a man who is leaving an unfinished work, and be reconciled ; and then come back and offer his gift. It is to be done quickly. This is emphasized in a second metaphor. In case of a debt you would have to act quickly, or the law would be in train and extreme consequences would follow. So in moral offences go quickly and satisfy ; purge your conscience and get free ; suffer no delay ; otherwise the moral consequences will be in train, and the issue inevitable, and the final result follow.

He speaks to Jews, but he also speaks to Christians. It is the law of the new kingdom. We have an altar. We have to offer up spiritual sacrifices, the worship of God in spirit and in truth. Thus in the course of the first century Jewish Christians apparently applied this saying of our Lord to the Holy Communion. In *The Doctrine of the Twelve Apostles* [1] you

---

[1] *Did.* xiv. 2.

find : " Let no man who has a dispute
with his fellow come together with you,
until they be reconciled [the word in
St. Matt. v. 24], that your sacrifice be not
defiled." Surely we need to lay to heart
this teaching, that we are to *make haste*
to get rid of whatever hinders our approach to God. We Englishmen are so
apt to pride ourselves on not being
hypocrites. It was once said to me, and
the saying has always remained in my
mind, that the great need in our day is
to preach against the Pharisaism of the
publican ! How many say, " I don't
come to the sacrament : a man who has
to knock about and make his way in the
world must do things and put up with
things which if one comes to the sacrament one is supposed to repent of. And
if I do not profess to be impossibly strict,
at least I am not a hypocrite." So he
goes off. " Lord, I thank thee that I
am not one of these hypocrites : I make
no religious professions, thank God ! "
Now this is what I call the Pharisaism of
the publican. Pharisaism is being satisfied
with ourselves. And the Pharisaism of
the man who makes no religious professions is at least as bad as the Pharisaism

of the man who abounds in them. Our
Lord does not bid us abstain from coming
to the altar if we are not fit, but He says,
See to it that you make yourselves fit ;
and that too in a hurry. " Leave there
thy gift before the altar," but you cannot
leave it long. It will be in the way there.
There is an unfinished work which you are
engaged in. Make haste to come back
and finish it. If among my readers are
some who belong to the Church and are
not communicants, and are satisfied because they are not hypocrites, I would
say to them—do not be satisfied : begin
to approach the altar : commit yourself
to it, by telling your wife or husband, or
friend or parish priest, that you hope to
receive the Communion, and when ; and
then go your ways quickly and remove
the moral obstacles which hinder your
doing so ; otherwise the moral train
will be set in motion, and the great and
inevitable issue come before you know
it.

There is one other point which I will ask
you to notice—our Lord's use in this
passage of the word " brother." In the
Bible the term " brother " is confined to
those who belong to the covenant ; in the

old law to the Jews, in the new law to the Christians. Our Lord then is here dealing with the relation of Christian to Christian, who have realized their brotherhood in the common fatherhood of God. All men are meant for brotherhood, but our Lord is speaking here to those who are brothers in fact.

THE LAW OF ADULTERY

" Ye have heard that it was said, Thou shalt not commit adultery : but I say unto you, that every one that looketh on a woman to lust after her hath committed adultery with her already in his heart."

We notice that our Lord here brings to light a fresh principle. In the case of the sixth commandment He notes the sin of allowing even the feeling of hatred ; but he *distinguishes* the guilt of an allowed *feeling*, not only from that of an act, but also from that of a word. But here our Lord *identifies* with the overt act in guilt even the desire of the heart when it reaches the point of deliberate *intention* to sin. The man whom our Lord is here considering must be supposed to have the deliberate intention to sin ; he looks on the woman *in order to* [1] excite his lust ;

---

[1] Cf. vi. 1, " in order to be seen of men," where the phrase is the same and describes the deliberate motive.

he is only restrained from action (if it be so) by lack of opportunity or fear of consequences ; in his will and intention he has already committed the act. Our Lord then says that to will to sin and deliberately to stimulate sin in oneself has in His sight all the guilt of sin, even though circumstances may restrain one from the actual commission of it. This again is a principle which applies to other commandments besides the seventh.

Then, in view of the difficulty of sexual purity, our Lord goes on to urge men to take those necessary steps in the way of self-discipline, which will enable them to be preserved from sin :

"And if thy right eye causeth thee to stumble, pluck it out, and cast it from thee : for it is profitable for thee that one of thy members should perish, and not thy whole body be cast into hell. And if thy right hand causeth thee to stumble, cut it off, and cast it from thee : for it is profitable for thee that one of thy members should perish, and not thy whole body go into hell."

Here our Lord lays down the important principle of asceticism or self-discipline, and we should carefully notice some points in His teaching about it.

1. What our Lord tells us is that a safe life is better than a complete life.

All parts of our nature were made by God. The best thing is that we should be able to exercise freely all our faculties ; but we must be safe at the centre before we can be free at the circumference. And if we find that any one of our faculties is so disordered in fact that it is destroying the roots of our life, we must be remorseless in limiting ourselves ; a limited life is better than a life insecure at the roots. Whatever exposes us to temptation that is too strong for us must at all costs be abandoned. Bengel says, with much insight, " How many there are who have been destroyed by neglecting the mortification of one single member."

This principle is easy of application to questions which are constantly coming up. Is it right to go to the theatre, or to this or that theatre ? Is this or that particular sort of art or literature legitimate and justifiable ? Now to a certain extent these questions can be answered on general principles. But it does not at all follow, because on general principles I can justify this or that drama, or this or that literature, or this or that kind of art, that therefore it is justified for me. That is quite another question. The

question for me is, what is its effect on
me? does it in me stimulate what is
bad? does it put my moral nature to a
disadvantage? does it in fact betray me
into sin? If so, I have no right at all
to excuse myself from abstinence on
general grounds—unless, indeed, I am
one of those people in whose case con-
scientiousness has a tendency to become
a morbid scrupulosity. In such cases of
mental disease the individual conscience
often needs rectifying by reference to a
more healthy common sense. But these
for the moment are not under consideration. The peril which our Lord has in
view is the more usual one of moral
carelessness. And His warning is very
solemn. Speaking of course in metaphor,
but speaking metaphor which means something terribly real, He says it is better
to live a maimed life than with all our
faculties about us to be destined to
moral death.

2. Here is the distinctive principle of
Christian asceticism. If we go to India,
we still find ascetics there whose asceticism
is based on the oriental idea that the
body is in itself an evil thing, and that
to be spiritual is to be separated from

material things. That is not the Christian
idea. The Christian idea is that the
whole of this material nature, including
our bodies, is good in itself and meant
to be consecrated to spiritual uses. We
are never to mortify any faculty as if it
were an evil thing to be got rid of. The
end of all Christian self-discipline is that
we may have the freedom of our whole
nature. But freedom is only possible
where there is rational control. Thus
any sacrifice is worth making sooner
than that the lower part of our nature
should lord it over the higher.

Next, as a sequence to this treatment
of the seventh commandment, our Lord
deals with the question of divorce.

" It was said also, Whosoever shall put away his
wife, let him give her a writing of divorcement ;
but I say unto you, that every one that putteth
away his wife, saving for the cause of fornication,
maketh her an adulteress : and whosoever shall
marry her when she is put away committeth
adultery."

The Jewish law of divorce is given in
Deuteronomy xxiv. 1, 2 :

" When a man taketh a wife, and marrieth her,
then it shall be, if she find no favour in his eyes,
because he hath found some unseemly thing in her,
that he shall write her a bill of divorcement, and
give it in her hand, and send her out of his house.

And when she is departed out of his house, she may go and be another man's wife."

This, especially as interpreted in Jewish tradition, had given a great liberty of divorce, which our Lord here abolishes or restrains. What we may truly call His legislation on this subject is repeated in St. Matthew xix. 3–9 :

"And there came unto him Pharisees, tempting him, and saying, Is it lawful for a man to put away his wife for every cause ? And he answered and said, Have ye not read, that he which made them from the beginning made them male and female, and said, For this cause shall a man leave his father and mother, and shall cleave to his wife ; and the twain shall become one flesh? So that they are no more twain, but one flesh. What therefore God hath joined together, let not man put asunder. They say unto him, Why then did Moses command to give a bill of divorcement, and to put her away ? He saith unto them, Moses for your hardness of heart suffered you to put away your wives : but from the beginning it hath not been so. And I say unto you, Whosoever shall put away his wife, except for fornication, and shall marry another, committeth adultery : and he that marrieth her when she is put away committeth adultery."

Now leaving out of question the clause in both passages in which an exception seems to be made, we notice, first of all, that our Lord proclaimed, as a prominent law of His new kingdom, the indis-solubility of marriage. And for us as

Christians it is perfectly plain that not all the parliaments or kings on earth can alter the law of our Lord. And if any ministers of Christ, or persons claiming to represent the Church of Christ, ever dare to let the commandment of men, in however high places, override the law of Christ, they are simply behaving in a way which brings them under the threat which our Lord so solemnly uttered: " Whosoever shall be ashamed of me and of my words in this adulterous and sinful generation, the Son of Man also shall be ashamed of him, when he cometh in the glory of his Father with the holy angels." [1] Beyond all question, for the Church, and for all who desire to call themselves Christians, it is absolutely out of the question to regard those as married who, having been divorced, have been married again, contrary to the law of Christ, during the lifetime of their former partner. It is quite true that this indissolubility of marriage may press hardly upon individuals in exceptional cases. But so does every law which is for the welfare of mankind in general ; and, press it hardly or softly, the words of

[1] St. Mark viii. 38.

our Lord are quite unmistakable. He who refused to legislate on so many subjects legislated on this, and the simple question arises whether we prefer the authority of Christ to any other authority whatever.

But, secondly, our Lord appears in both passages to make an exception, and the exception would seem to sanction, or, more strictly, not to prohibit, the re-marriage of an innocent man who has put away his wife for adultery.

Various attempts have been made to obviate the force of this exception. But to the present writer they do not commend themselves as at all satisfactory.[1] Chiefly it is pleaded that the exception does not appear in St. Luke's Gospel or in St. Paul's epistles where marriage is dealt with. But it is a law of interpretation that a command with a specific qualification is more precise than a general command without any specific qualification ; and that the one where the qualification occurs must interpret the other where this qualification does not occur.[2]

---

[1] See App. iii. p. 227. Duty of the Church with regard to divorce.

[2] And it cannot be overlooked that in one of the

We must recognize also that in the un-divided Church there was great difference of opinion on this subject, that in the Eastern Church at least the re-marriage of the innocent party has been allowed, and that, though not tolerated in the Western Church or in the canons of the English Church, the bishops of the Anglican communion assembled at Lambeth in 1888 have allowed its recognition. Their reso-lutions are as follows :—

" 1. That, inasmuch as our Lord's words expressly forbid divorce, except in the case of fornication or adultery, the Christian Church cannot recognize divorce in any other than the excepted case, or give any sanction to the marriage of any person who has been divorced contrary to this law, during the life of the other party.

2. That under no circumstances ought the guilty party, in the case of a divorce for fornication or adultery, to be regarded, during the lifetime of the innocent party, as a fit recipient of the blessing of the Church on marriage.

passages of St. Paul's epistles where the law of the indissolubility of marriage is stated (Romans vii. 1–3) he is referring to the *Jewish* law (see ver. 1) which con-fessedly admitted exceptions, and yet he does not allude to them.

3. That, recognizing the fact that there always has been a difference of opinion in the Church on the question whether our Lord meant to forbid marriage to the innocent party in a divorce for adultery, the Conference recommends that the clergy should not be instructed to refuse the sacraments or other privileges of the Church to those who, under civil sanction, are thus married."

I have dealt only with the interpretation of St. Matthew's Gospel ; not directly with the present duty of English churchmen. But there is perhaps no matter which threatens so seriously the peace of the Church of England as this matter of divorce. And I venture to state my own view of the best way to meet the difficulty.

I have stated above that the unaltered law of the *Church* of England—as distinct from the *State*—allows no exception to the indissolubility of marriage. Those who assent to the interpretation of the passages in St. Matthew's Gospel which has just been given, will recognize that the church law of England might be modified in the sense of the Lambeth decisions without any disloyalty to Christ.

But it has not been modified, and, as it stands, it ought to control our action. Moreover in the present state of feeling, in view of our present social experiences, and of the difficulty of maintaining the distinction between the innocent and guilty party, it is probably undesirable to attempt to modify it by canon. The best course, in my judgement, is to maintain the existing church law by refusing to allow any re-marriage, even of the innocent party in a divorce for adultery, with the rites or in the consecrated buildings of the Church. This would still leave it open for bishops to act upon the third clause of the recommendation of the Lambeth Conference, and to instruct their clergy to admit to communion such " innocent parties " as have been re-married under civil sanction.

THE LAW OF TAKING AN OATH

" Again, ye have heard that it was said to them of old time, Thou shalt not forswear thyself, but shalt perform unto the Lord thine oaths : but I say unto you, Swear not at all ; neither by the heaven, for it is the throne of God ; nor by the earth, for it is the footstool of his feet ; nor by Jerusalem, for it is the city of the great King. Neither shalt thou swear by thy head, for thou canst not make one hair white or black. But let your speech be, Yea, yea ; Nay, nay : and whatsoever is more than these is of the evil one."

The third commandment, taken with other passages of the Old Testament,[1] enjoined upon the Israelite to swear only by the name of Jehovah ; and so swearing, to be diligent to perform his oath. And our Lord both restores the injunction [2] and deepens it.

What, we ask, is the nature of an oath ? It is for a man to put himself solemnly in God's presence, and assert that, as surely as God is God, and as he hopes for His blessing on his life, what he is saying is the truth. The essence of the oath is the solemnly putting oneself *on special occasions* in the presence of God. But is not God everywhere present ? Are we ever out of His presence ? Does not everything live simply with His life and depend on His will ? Is there then any meaning in selecting set occasions to put ourselves in God's presence, when God is always present and all that exists exists in Him ? It is to this truth of the omnipresence and omnipotence of

---

[1] Lev. xix. 12 ; Deut. vi. 13 ; Amos viii. 14.
[2] St. Matt. xxiii. 16–20.

God that our Lord calls men's attention ;
and He deals with the Jewish commandment by lifting all conversation, all use
of language, in His new kingdom to the
level which had previously been held
by declarations on oath.   To the Jew it
had been a great thing to forswear himself,
but little or nothing to speak in ordinary
talk what was not true.   Our Lord says :
God is everywhere and all words are
uttered in His presence ;   therefore truth
is of universal obligation ;   your yea is
always to be yea, and your nay, nay.

Not only have we in St. James' Epistle [1]
a repetition of this injunction of our
Lord, when it was much needed, but
we have an instructive comment upon
it in the distress which it occasioned St.
Paul to be accused unjustly of prevarica-
tion and untruth to his promise.[2]   Truth
to his word is to be always and everywhere the characteristic of a Christian.
It is not to be at one time " yea, yea,"
and at another time " nay, nay."   How
fundamentally the absence of this characteristic of mutual trustworthiness can
hinder social progress among Christians
is, I fear, apparent at the present day

[1] Ch. v. 12.   [2] 2 Cor. i. 17, 18.

in the case of those whom (by a limitation of the term equally unfortunate for those who are included in it, and for those who are not) we call the working-classes.

In this connexion we may notice three points.

1. The duty of truthfulness comes under the third commandment as deepened by our Lord. In questions for self-examination on the Ten Commandments, as interpreted for Christians, one almost always sees the duty of truthfulness brought under the ninth. But that, in view of our Lord's words, is certainly wrong, and is due originally to a tendency to depreciate the sinfulness of lying, except where wrong appears to be done by it to the reputation or interests of another. Our Lord brings untruthfulness of all kinds under the prohibition of the third commandment simply by deepening its fundamental principle.

2. Though our Lord teaches God's omnipresence, yet He none the less recognizes degrees of His presence. We very often hear objections made, if we allege a special presence of God in the church, or at the altar in the Holy Communion. Is not God, it is asked, present every-

4

where ? Yes ; " heaven is God's *throne* ;
the earth is His *footstool* ; Jerusalem is
His *city*." [1] Just because God's presence
is not physical, but spiritual, therefore
it admits degrees of intensity. God is
everywhere present ; but He is present
in a special way and for a special purpose
where two or three are gathered together ; and, again, in a special way and
for a special purpose in the ordinances of
His sacramental grace. Similarly He is,
we may say, more present in rational
beings than in irrational ; and in good
men more than in bad.

3. We must answer the question—Are
all oaths prohibited to the Christian ?
is it always wrong for a Christian to
go into a court of justice and be sworn ?
Our Lord Himself, we notice, consented
to be put on oath by the high priest—
" I adjure thee by God,"—and to that
adjuration He answered.[2] And on three
or four occasions St. Paul takes God to
witness, and says, in effect, As God is
my witness, this is true. With these
precedents, I do not think it is possible
to say a Christian may not take an oath
in a court of justice, or difficult to explain

[1] Is. lxvi. 1 ; Ps. lviii. 2.   [2] St. Matt. xxvi. 63.

why he may. It is for this reason. When a Christian goes to take an oath in a court of law he should only go to profess openly that motive to truthfulness which rules all his speech. Even so, the need that he should take an oath comes of the habitual neglect of truth in ordinary conversation : in this sense any taking of an oath " is of the evil one." And a man is quite below the Christian standard who thinks himself bound to truth by his oath, but not by his word in common speech. What are we to say then of the universally attested fact that even perjury, or false swearing, is in the law-courts of our Christian country a quite ordinary occurrence ?

CHAPTER V

AFTER dealing thus with three of the
Ten Commandments our Lord proceeds
to deal with two other prescriptions or
ideas of the old covenant. As He had
done to the commandments, He deepens
and intensifies them till they reach that
standard which commends itself to His
holy and perfect mind. In both cases
our Lord's treatment of the older moral
standard is both profoundly interesting
and at the same time the cause of no little
difficulty and scruple to Christian consciences.

THE LAW OF REVENGE

" Ye have heard that it was said, An eye for an
eye, and a tooth for a tooth :. but I say unto you,
Resist not him that is evil : but whosoever smiteth
thee on thy right cheek, turn to him the other also.
And if any man would go to law with thee, and take
away thy coat, let him have thy cloke also. And
whosoever shall compel thee to go one mile, go with

him twain. Give to him that asketh thee, and from him that would borrow of thee turn not thou away."

Our Lord is here dealing with one interesting prescription of the old law. It had definitely allowed revenge up to a certain point, but no further. It might go to the point of exact reciprocity. So the law in Exodus xxi. 24, 25 lays it down : "Eye for eye, tooth for tooth, hand for hand, foot for foot, burning for burning, wound for wound, stripe for stripe."

1. Here we must remark, first, that the law of the old covenant was in itself a limitation of human instinct. The savage instinct of revenge is to rush blindly in, and do as much harm to an enemy as can be done. The savage satisfies himself to the full ; he kills the man that has done him wrong and his wife and family. Now nothing is more striking in the old covenant than that it checks barbarous habits and puts them under restraint. It is so with the habit of animal sacrifice ; it is so in the law of revenge. The Mosaic law stands by, as it were, as a policeman, and says, An eye ? is that the wrong done ? Then an eye may be put out in return ; but no more. You must stop there. The point which needs emphasizing is that

the old law worked by way of gradual limitation, not of sudden abolition. God dealt with men gradually. Their savage passions are restrained under the Old Testament as a preparation for the time when they were to be brought under the perfect discipline of the Son of Man. So now, when the fullness of the time is come, our Lord lays on this passion of revenge à harder and deeper prescription, and says in fact to each of His disciples : A wrong aimed at thee as an individual is, so far as thy feeling goes, simply to be an occasion for showing complete liberty of spirit and superiority to all outrage. The Lord requires not moderation in revenge, but complete self-efface-ment.

2. Secondly, we may notice that this requirement of self-effacement is of the nature of an ascetic prescription, as when our Lord said " If thy right eye offend thee, pluck it out ; if thy right hand offend thee, cut it off." The necessity for this self-mutilation—cutting off a hand, pluck-ing out an eye—lay in the fact that these limbs, or faculties, or functions of our nature had been so utterly misused that before they could be again used

legitimately they must be put under this stern discipline of effacement.

So with this instinct of revenge. The instinct has in it something that is right : something of the passion of justice. It is a true instinct which makes us feel that for wrong done man should suffer wrong. It is derived from the divine principle of justice. But in our own cases, where our own interests are concerned, this passion of justice has come to be so mixed up with selfishness, and with those excessive demands which spring of selfishness—in a word, it has become so defiled with sin—that our Lord imposes on it an absolute ban ; He says " Vengeance is mine, I will repay, saith the Lord." He takes away from us, as it were, the right to administer justice in our own case. " The wrath of man worketh not the righteousness of God." [1] He requires us as individuals to acknowledge the law of self-effacement.

3. The requirement which our Lord lays on His disciples is not only made in words. It was enforced, where the enforcement is most striking, in our Lord's example. You watch our Lord in His

[1] St. James i. 20.

passion ; and when you look delicately
and accurately at the details of the
treatment He received, you observe how
almost intolerably hard to bear were
many of His trials. We can hardly conceive what to Him it must have been to
bear the hideous insults and injustices
of men. Think for example, to take a
subtle but impressive instance,[1] of those
false accusations brought against Him
which had in them the sound of truth.
" And there stood up certain, and bear
false witness against him, saying, We
heard him say, I will destroy this temple
that is made with hands, and in three
days I will build another made without
hands." [2] He had said in fact not that,
but something like it. He had said
" Destroy this temple, and in three days
I will raise it up." [3] That is, Suppose
you destroy, then I will rebuild. There
was a great difference between what He
had said and what He was accused of
saying. But you know in what atmo-
sphere it is that such accusations are
brought. The crowd does not consider

---

[1] I owe this thought, I believe, to an address given
by the Dean of Chichester.
[2] St. Mark xiv. 57–8.   [3] St. John ii. 19.

details ; it listens to the vague sound of
the words ; it is easily convinced : " He
said something of that sort. If he defends
himself, he has to quibble." And thus
they rush off and put down to the accused
man not what he said, but what he was
supposed to have said. Now our Lord
had that delicate instinct of the pastor.
He knew there were people watching
Him, and wondering whether He were
the true Messiah or no. To have an
accusation brought against Him which
sounded as if true, and, though it was
not true, excited such fierce animosity
against Him—this was a profound trial
of spirit : and it is only one instance
in which a little imagination, if we bring
it to bear, shows us the depth of what
our Lord had to endure not only in the
way of insults, but of injustices. Yet
" when he was reviled, he reviled not
again ; when he suffered, he threatened
not ; but committed himself to him that
judgeth righteously." [1]

4. When our own personal feeling has
been utterly suppressed, then it is quite
possible that another duty, the duty of
justice, the duty of maintaining the social

[1] 1 St. Peter ii. 23.

4*

order, may come into prominence again.
Thus our Lord is in another passage [1]
recorded to have said something that
may appear at first sight plainly contradictory to what He says here. " If
thy brother sin against thee "—are you
simply to take no notice of it ? No.
You are to " shew him his fault between
thee and him alone : if he hear thee,
thou hast gained thy brother. But if
he hear thee not, take with thee one
or two more, that at the mouth of two
witnesses or three every word may be
established. And if he refuse to hear
them, tell it unto the church : and if
he refuse to hear the church also, let
him be unto thee as the Gentile and
the publican."

Here it is obvious our Lord is enjoining
not an extreme measure of personal
meekness, but an extreme insistence on
social justice. And He Himself made
a certain claim on justice in His trial :
" And when he had said this, one of
the officers standing by struck Jesus
with his hand, saying, Answerest thou
the high priest so ? Jesus answered him,
If I have spoken evil, bear witness of

[1] St. Matt. xviii. 15.

the evil : but if well, why smitest thou me ? " [1] So St. Paul, in the Acts of the Apostles, claims justice : " I am standing before Cæsar's judgement-seat, where I ought to be judged : to the Jews have I done no wrong, as thou also very well knowest. If then I am a wrong-doer, and have committed anything worthy of death, I refuse not to die : but if none of those things is true, whereof these accuse me, no man can give me up unto them. I appeal unto Cæsar." [2]

We observe therefore two opposite duties. There is the clear duty, so far as mere personal feeling goes, of simple self-effacement. Only then, when we have got our own wills thoroughly subordinated to God's will, when all the wild instinct of revenge is subdued, are we in a position to consider the other duty and to ask ourselves what the maintenance of the moral order of society may require of us.

This particular point gives us an opportunity to consider generally our Lord's method in teaching. We have been

[1] St. John xviii. 22–23.
[2] Acts xxv. 10–11, cf. xvi. 37.

brought up against one conspicuous instance in which our Lord appears to
contradict Himself ; and the explanation
of this lies in His method. At times
we must notice His method was metaphorical. When we were considering
what He says about asceticism, for example, we saw that the instances given
were plainly metaphorical. " If thine eye
offend thee, pluck it out and cast it
from thee." That is a metaphor for
violently putting under restraint any
faculty which has been misused.

But here His instances are not metaphorical. They are such as quite admit
of actual and literal application. They
are, however, *proverbial*. You may notice
in the proverbs of all nations that they
easily admit of appearing to be contradictory and yet of being perfectly
intelligible in the guidance they give us.
One day you will hear a man condemned
as " penny wise and pound foolish " ;
another day it is " take care of the
pence, and the pounds will take care
of themselves." One day it is " look
before you leap " ; another " nothing
venture, nothing have." The suggestions
involved in these pairs of proverbs are

contradictory. The important matter according to the one is to be careful about large sums, according to the other to be careful about small sums : according to one to think before you act, according to the other to be ready to run a risk. But each gives what is obviously the right guidance to certain characters in certain situations, and gives it after the manner of proverbs. A proverb embodies a principle of common, but not universal, application in an absolute and extreme form. Another proverb may embody another principle in a similar form. And thus expressed they may easily appear contradictory, and both alike impracticable, if taken literally, because all the qualifying circumstances are left out.

Our Lord then teaches by proverbs. In emphasizing one principle He expresses it as an absolute direction in an extreme instance : " If a man will take thy coat, let him have thy cloke also." In emphasizing another principle He expresses it in a similar form : " If thy brother trespass against thee, go and tell him his fault " and follow the matter up to its extreme consequences.

And every one must recognize that the right application of each proverb depends on the question, What is the particular principle which at a particular moment is to be brought into play ? No proverb could be ever taken as a rule for constant action, but only as a type of action when a particular principle is to be expressed.

Now we may take the injunctions which our Lord gives, and ask ourselves how we can apply these particular proverbs to-day.

" But I say unto you, Resist not him that is evil: but whosoever smiteth thee on thy right cheek, turn to him the other also."

The actual words need of course no explanation. But can we see how we are to apply the precept ? would it " do " to obey it exactly and literally ? Well, there are occasions when it might be obeyed, if not literally—because people may seldom, or perhaps never, smite us on the right cheek—yet nearly literally ; occasions when nothing is concerned but our own instinct of revenge or our own pride, and we had better simply take meekly some insult or wrong, and make no effort to defend ourselves.

For example : there is a nasty thing said about you in the newspaper or a nasty thing whispered about you in the circle where you move, and you know quite well who has put it into the newspaper or given it currency. You cannot be mistaken ; there is evidence ; only one person could have done it. And the statement made is really untrue. No one can be subjected to that kind of wrong, without being brought face to face with the question whether he intends to be a thorough-going Christian. For there is no doubt what we ought to do. We ought not to be content till we have utterly crushed out of ourselves the least desire, as far as our own personal feeling is concerned, to take any kind of revenge whatever. We are to efface ourselves utterly, we are to turn the other cheek. That means, of course, that we decline to show in any way that we know who has done the wrong, and that we are at pains to look out for an opportunity of kindness to the person who has wronged us. That would be not a literal but a practical application of the principle, and there are numerous occasions in any man's life when it is right to act thus, and any other course of conduct at all is more or less morally wrong, because no social duty compels us to assert our just cause.

The next injunction is :

"And if any man would go to law with thee, and take away thy coat, let him have thy cloke also."

There again, it is quite plain what is meant. It is to refuse to resist legal injustice. Very often it can and ought to be literally obeyed. " Nay, already it is altogether a defect in you, that ye have lawsuits one with another. Why not rather take wrong ? why not rather be defrauded ? "[1] But there are also instances in which to act literally on this precept would be, in any sober judgement, doing a great wrong to society and to the man who is himself the wrong doer. But the question is, am I able to look at the matter from that point of view ? The difficulty to almost all of us is to get into such a state of mind that we can honestly say, As far as my own will goes, I am ready to suffer this and more ; and not to let the question of legal proceedings come into our minds

[1] 1 Cor. vi. 7.

at all till we are sure that our motive is the general interest of society and of the wrong doer.

Then, once more:

> "And whosoever shall compel thee to go one mile, go with him twain."

There was a public transport service which passed from the Persian into later empires. Our Lord then says "When any public officer presses thee into the transport service for a certain way, be prepared to take double the impost." That is—do not resent public claims upon you, bear the public burdens, and be willing that, as far as you are concerned, they should be double what they are. But how we dislike the rates and taxes! How few there are who take a Christian view of paying them, and are glad, up to their means, to accept the burden which membership in this great nation lays upon them. Something more is our duty than to make barely honest returns for an income tax.

> "Give to him that asketh thee," and (in St. Luke) "of him that taketh away thy goods ask them not again."

Probably most of us know the old

sculpture on the back of the screen behind the high altar in our abbey of Westminster. It is one of those in which are represented the traditions about our (almost) patron saint, Edward the Confessor. The king is resting after the labours of the day, and Hugolin, his chamberlain, has brought out the chest of money to pay his various retainers. But he leaves it open while he is out of the way ; a scullion comes in, and thinking the king is asleep, twice he carries off treasure out of the chest. While he is enriching himself the third time, the king, who has seen all, quietly observes : " Fly, fellow, as quickly as you can, for Hugolin is coming back, and he will not leave you so much as a half-penny." Hugolin does come, and, finding out what has occurred, questions the king. The king however will not disclose who has taken the treasure : " He needed it more than we ; Edward has surely enough treasure. As Jesus Christ teaches us, worldly property ought to be common to all those who have need of it." [1]

[1] The story is given from a Norman-French poem of the time of Henry III, probably by a Westminster monk ; see *Lives of Edward the Confessor*, Rolls Series, iii. pp. 53, 207.

We need not doubt that occasions still occur when even fantastic acts of generosity, such as this, are the things needed to make an impression on hardened or embittered or careless hearts. Every one knows Victor Hugo's story of the bishop and the convict in *Les Miserables*, and no doubt it represents realities in life and experience.

On the whole, however, it is seldom that it would be right to let the thief have his own way. But it is always right to deal very mercifully with first offences and to take trouble to give the offenders a clear fresh chance. And even if the law is let to take its course with a criminal, yet kindness to him while he is suffering his sentence and after it—kindness which does not shrink from taking a great deal of trouble— can produce the same moral impression as a literal application of the divine proverb like King Edward's.

"Give to him that asketh thee, and from him that would borrow of thee, turn not thou away."

What are we to say to the beggar, of whatever grade ? Now, first of all, there are a great many cases where help is needed, and "asked for" therefore, whether by a spoken or an unspoken appeal, by people of whom we know the character and circumstances antecedently. Misfortunes happen to people who are such as can profitably be helped, that is, such as when they are helped in a temporary difficulty will be enabled to resume the normal course of a self-helping life : or such as will need permanent help indeed, as they are permanently incapacitated, but have the will and character to work. Or there are cases where help can be given to educate a young man or woman for the priesthood or some other honourable career. There are in fact no lack of cases in which we can with the greatest profit help individuals, and that largely and generously, to say nothing of innumerable societies and institutions which need and ask, but find few to give regularly and bountifully. This sort of regular generosity costs us much more than giving coppers to beggars or shillings to applicants by post. " Let thine alms sweat into thine hand, until thou knowest to whom thou shouldest give," was the advice given in a very early Christian community.[1]

[1] *Didache* 1. It must not be forgotten that both St.

Next, let us take notice that we can
" make inquiries." People shrink from
this because it takes trouble and implies
methodical principles. But there is no
equally secure means of sifting out cases
of honest need from those of professional
begging. The " professionals" will not
come near a house where it is known
that inquiries are made. And the fact
that we take kindly trouble about them,
should appeal to what is good in any
man's conscience.

But as to indiscriminate charity ? It
has been encouraged very often by the
teachers of Christianity.[1] But if a tree
is known by its fruits, the system is all
condemned. It is in fact an indulgence
of our feelings of compassion, with little
trouble to ourselves, and at the expense
of society. To give indeed to any beggar
the plainest broken food may do no

John (1 John iii. 17) and St. James (ii. 15–16) are speaking
of helping " a brother " or " sister," i.e. a fellow-Chris-
tian. And in those days there was an immense proba-
bility that a member of the Christian society would
be one who had character enough to profit by help.
But it soon became necessary to " organize charity"
by desiring the faithful to give only indirectly through
the bishop.

[1] From the days of the sub-apostolic Hermas, who
makes the responsibility rest wholly with the recipient
of alms.

harm. But it is very seldom welcomed.
Again we can do something to indicate
friendly, kindly feeling towards an applicant, if we take pains. Perhaps, for
instance, we can get a boy-beggar on
to a training ship. At least, so far as
we can, let us not resent taking trouble
about people who have no " special claim"
on us. And when our Christian judgement can approve it, let us not resent
expense. Let our whole conduct make
it evident that we welcome and do not
resent claims either on our purse, or
on our heart, or on our intelligence.
But our intelligence must be brought
to bear upon our charity as well as
our heart. To illustrate how this is
forgotten I will only repeat a story of
the saintly William Law. He seems to
have distributed as much as £2,500 a
year, chiefly in doles to applicants who
came into his back yard ; he succeeded
in getting rid of his money, and in de-
moralizing the neighbourhood.[1] But it
is plainly not our Lord's will that we
should do manifest harm.

Indiscriminate charity is not enjoined,
but a self-sacrificing generosity is. And

[1] Overton's *Life and Opinions of W. Law*, p. 244.

it would be well if every Christian who is wealthy or " comfortably-off " would, before passing on from this passage, kneel upon his knees as in God's presence and ask himself if he is making a serious attempt to accept loyally the claim upon his time and money which his Lord makes on behalf of those who want.

THE TREATMENT OF ENEMIES

" Ye have heard that it was said, Thou shalt love thy neighbour, and hate thine enemy : but I say unto you, Love your enemies, and pray for them that persecute you ; that ye may be sons of your Father which is in heaven : for he maketh his sun to rise on the evil and the good, and sendeth rain on the just and the unjust. For if ye love them that love you, what reward have ye ? do not even the publicans the same ? And if ye salute your brethren only, what do ye more than others ? do not even the Gentiles the same ? Ye therefore shall be perfect, as your heavenly Father is perfect."

The exact expression, " Thou shalt hate thine enemy," nowhere occurs in the Mosaic law ; and there are, both in the law and elsewhere in the Old Testament, passages which come nearer to the Christian standard.[1] But on the whole we must accept Dr. Mozley's conclusion : [2] " The whole precept as it

[1] e.g. Job xxxi. 29 ; Exod. xxiii. 4.
[2] *Lectures on the O.T.* viii. 2, p. 188.

stands undoubtedly represents, and is a summary of, the sense of the law " : nor can " the enemy " be regarded as meaning *only* the enemies of Israel. Thus many Christian consciences are distressed while psalms are being sung in our services which contain imprecations upon enemies, such as the 109th. Some modern critics assure us that these psalms express no individual feelings towards personal enemies, but the feeling of righteous Israel towards the enemies of the Lord. It may be doubted whether this is altogether the case. And even if it is so, the psalms still fall short of the Christian standard both of hope for the conversion of enemies and of love toward them in any case. No doubt, if we take the Righteous One who speaks in them to be Christ, we can find in them the divine principles of judgement ; and so they are interpreted in the New Testament. Still in their mode of expression, and in the temper which they historically represent, they fall short of the Christian standard. And this ought not to surprise us. The whole Old Testament is on right lines of divine development : but it has not reached the goal, which is

Christ. "It was said to them of old . . . but I say unto you."

Our Lord, in deepening and widening the Old Testament law of love, inculcates kindliness in disposition, in word, in act. In disposition, we are to " love our enemies." Not of course that we can feel alike towards all people ; but we can set our will, or what the Bible calls our heart, to do them good. And if we dispose ourselves aright towards others, we shall probably end by feeling aright, though that can never be a matter of commandment. And we are to show our disposition towards them by kindly salutations, or the ordinary words which express human goodwill, and by deeds, both earnest prayer for them and acts which imitate the impartial beneficence of our Father in heaven.

Nothing is said about the effect which such kindness to professed enemies may have. But there is no question that if we treat people as if they were permanently and necessarily what they are at the moment, we fix or do our best to fix them in their present condition. To make people better, we must believe that God intends them to be better and treat them as if we believed them in fact to be better than they are. The clever barrister, Sidney Carton, in Dickens' *Tale of Two Cities*, who had been his own enemy, who had fallen from bad to worse, who had ceased to believe in himself as his friends also had ceased to believe in him, was recovered by a good and merciful woman who refused to take him at the general estimate and would not give him up—recovered, after many relapses, to the point of a final act of heroism by which he lost his own life to save his true friend's husband. So if we refuse to treat people as our enemies, we have the best possible chance of winning them to be our friends. God has redeemed men by treating them, not as they are, but as they are capable of becoming.

Our Lord calls our attention to the fact that He is requiring such conduct of us as only a supernatural motive, the motive of fellowship with God, can account for. This is a consideration which we can apply to other parts of Christian duty—for instance, to the obligation of purity. But our Lord here applies it to kindliness. " You are kind to your friends. Are not the publicans the same ? " The publicans proper were capitalists who " farmed " the Roman taxes, undertaking to hand over a certain sum for a certain district and then getting as much as they could out of the inhabitants. But the name was also applied to their subordinates, the custom-house officers, as in the New Testament. These were held in special odium by their countrymen and generally justified a character for rapacity. But even such men are kind to their friends. It requires no other motive than human convenience, the most ordinary social virtue. But what our Lord asks of us is something which requires the supernatural or divine motive to account for it. Here then we have a serious question. Consider your actions, your ordinary dealings with others. Are they such as can be accounted for by convenience and social requirement, or does your conduct require the divine motive, the motive of fellowship with God, to explain it and to make it possible ? It is only this latter sort of conduct that makes it—so to speak—worth while that Jesus Christ should have come down from heaven and sacrificed Himself for you. Are you walking worthily of the vocation wherewith ye are called ? For your principle of conduct is to be nothing less than a real striving after the perfection of God, which is indeed the character of Christ.

"Ye therefore shall be perfect, as your heavenly Father is perfect."

Yet we must not despair. We have Christ's Spirit working within us to make us like Christ : and if only we have the right ideal in front of us and are moving however slowly towards it, or even constantly recurring to the pursuit of it, we shall be perfected at last. We have eternity before us to grow in—not a year or two, or a life-time, but eternity. And in our best moments we do really recognize that what is most worth having in the world is the character of Christ. Only in proportion as we feel the magnitude of what is asked of us, let us throw ourselves upon the divine readiness to give strength and wisdom according to our needs. Let us pray with Augustine " Give what Thou commandest and then command what Thou willest."

CHAPTER VI

THE MOTIVE OF THE CITIZENS OF THE KINGDOM OF HEAVEN

WHEN we were considering the way in which our Lord deepens the law of love, while abrogating the law of revenge, we were obliged to notice that what He gives us is not literal enactments, but rather principles or motives for action. He expresses Himself indeed proverbially, in the form of particular injunctions or prohibitions. But the proverbial nature of these directions is apparent, in part because they are sometimes mutually contradictory; and they must be taken, like proverbs generally, as embodying in extreme concrete instances general principles or motives for action.

We may truly say that the Sermon on the Mount gives us a social law for Christians. That is true in this sense: the Sermon on the Mount gives us principles of action which every Christian must apply and re-apply in his social conduct. But just because it embodies motives and principles and does not give legal enactments, it must appeal in the first instance to the individual, to his heart and conscience ; and it is only as the character thus formed must set itself to remodel social life on a fresh basis, that the Sermon on the Mount can become a social law for Christians. You cannot take any one of its prescriptions, and apply it as a social law at once. You cannot take the maxim " If a man smite thee on the one cheek, turn to him the other also," or " If a man take away thy coat, let him have thy cloke also," and make it obligatory on Christians as a rule of external conduct, without upsetting the whole basis of society and without ignoring a contrary maxim which our Lord gives us in another connexion.

But each of the maxims can be taken to the heart and conscience of the individual, to become a principle of each man's own character and conduct, and then to reappear, retranslated into social action, according to the wisdom of the time or the wisdom of the man or the wisdom of the Church.

This truth—that our Lord is giving us principles, not laws—will appear only more conspicuously now, when we pass to the next great section of the Sermon ; because it will be obvious that our Lord can only be dealing with motives of action —motives such as belong to the secret heart of the individual. He proceeds to inculcate the abandonment of a worldly temper by prohibiting, literally, such religious actions as other men can see. But His own example, His own institution of a corporate religion, His special promises to common worship, His counter-maxim " Let your light so shine before men, that they may see your good works," force us to recognize the proverbial character of these prohibitions, and to look for the principle rather than the law.

And indeed this sixth chapter of St. Matthew's Gospel has one subject throughout. It teaches us one great principle— that the new righteousness, the righteousness of the citizens of the kingdom, looks throughout towards God. God is its motive, God is its aim, God is its object ; God, and nothing lower than God. No man is truly a citizen who is not in all his conduct and life looking directly God-ward.

We will attend first to verses 1–18, omitting the positive directions about prayer. Their theme does not vary : The Christian righteousness, in all its departments, looks for divine praise ; never for human praise. Our Lord lays this down first of righteousness generally, then of its different branches. Thus, in the first place, of righteousness generally :

"Take heed that ye do not your righteousness before men, to be seen of them : else ye have no reward with your Father which is in heaven."

We may observe here, once for all, that our Lord in no way disparages the seeking a reward, only the seeking it in a wrong place. There are " altruists " who regard the seeking of even an eternal reward from God as ignoble ; they would find the true religious motive only in such an utterance as that of St. Francis Xavier, "My God, I love Thee, not because I hope for heaven thereby," and would recall the mediæval story of the man who would quench with water the flames of hell and burn up with fire the joys of heaven, that men might seek God for His own sake. But indeed these philosophers ignore indestructible and necessary instincts in human nature. We cannot separate love

for God from a desire to find our own
happiness in God. This is inseparable
from personality. We must crave for
ultimate satisfaction, recognition, approval. The point is that we should seek
it in the right place, that is from God.
For coming from Him it can never involve any spoiling of our own capacity
for usefulness to others, or narrowing
of our own selves. Thus there is a true
self-love : and a true self-love seeks
satisfaction in the fellowship of God
in the eternal world. If " other-worldli-
ness " or the seeking of the divine reward
has done harm in religion, that is because
the character of the God whom we seek,
as revealed in the character and teaching
of Jesus Christ, has not been attended
to. Granted that we seek God as He is,
there can be no possible peril of our
undervaluing this world or the bodies
of men, nor of our tolerating selfishness in
religion. He that said " What is a man
profited if he shall gain the whole world and
lose his own life (soul) ? " said also, " He
that saveth his life (soul) shall lose it."

Then our Lord applies the general
principle of seeking only God's approval
to the three great branches of human

5

conduct. Christian, and indeed human conduct generally, looks in three directions. There is a duty to God, there is a duty to one's neighbour, and there is a duty to one's self. And each of these great departments of human conduct has one typical form of action, one form of action in which it specially expresses itself. Our duty to God expresses itself particularly in prayer. Our duty to man expresses itself in works of mercy, or alms. Our duty towards ourselves expresses itself in self-subdual, self-mastery—that is, fasting. And so our Lord applies the general principle to each of these typical duties. In your prayers, in your alms, in your fastings— in each case you are to look to nothing lower than the praise of God.

And, before we study these passages, let me ask you to notice how simply our Lord does always regard human life as bound to move in these three directions. There is our duty to God. That He puts first, not to be merged in our duty to our neighbour. There is our personal duty to God as a person, and it is the first and chief commandment to love the Lord our God. Then there is our duty towards our neighbour ; and then, also, there is our duty towards ourselves. " Thou shalt love thy neighbour —as thyself ! " Our duty towards ourselves is, in a word, to make the best of ourselves. Each one is an instrument, divinely created by God, with that sum total of faculties which the Bible calls his life or soul. Well, he is to make the best of himself. Considered as a spiritual being, capable of right spiritual activity, each man is to love himself and his neighbour and God ; himself, by bringing his whole being into good order and efficiency, which cannot be without fasting or the subdual of the flesh to the spirit : his neighbour, by considering his true interests like his own, which cannot be without almsgiving or actual gifts out of his substance to supply the other's needs : and God, which cannot be unless he deal with Him as a person by way of actual personal requests in prayer. And in each direction he is to seek only the praise of God.

ALMSGIVING

" When therefore thou doest alms, sound not a trumpet before thee, as the hypocrites do in the

synagogues and in the streets, that they may have
glory of men.   Verily I say unto you, They have
received their reward.   But when thou doest alms,
let not thy left hand know what thy right hand
doeth : that thine alms may be in secret : and thy
Father which seeth in secret shall recompense thee."

Our Lord is clearly using a metaphor.
We cannot suppose that the Jews, when
they went to give alms, caused their
own trumpet to be blown in a literal
sense ;   and in the same way, when
our Lord speaks of the left hand not
knowing what the right hand doeth, it
is clearly a metaphor ;   but a metaphor
vividly descriptive.   For what our Lord
is here forbidding is obviously ostentation
in doing good.

Here is a matter upon which it is for
each man to examine himself.   We are
to find out what our *motive* is.   We are
not to be troubled because, when we
are trying to do good, there comes across
us the temptation to think that people
are looking at us.   We shall often be
tempted in this way :   but the point is,
what is our motive ?   We can find that
out.   When people are not looking at
us, do we stop doing the good action ?
When we cannot be seen, do we omit it ?
If not, let us not be worried because we

may be tempted with thoughts of vain-glory. You know what an old saint said to Satan : " Not for thy sake did I begin this ; and not for thy sake shall I leave it off." But on the other hand, if you give a half-crown in a collection when there is a plate, and a penny when there is a bag and your gift cannot be seen ; or if you put yourself down for a larger sum in a subscription list in order to be brought into association with a duchess, then you have the gravest possible reason to doubt your motive.

And let me add this : there are many charitable people who desire to collect money for good objects ; let them take care that in order to do so they do not encourage people in bad motives. If they play upon bad motives to get money, assuredly they are partakers of other men's sins : and the money is not to the glory of God or for the good of His work.

Prayer

" And when ye pray, ye shall not be as the hypo-crites : for they love to stand and pray in the syna-gogues and in the corners of the streets, that they may be seen of men. Verily I say unto you, They have received their reward. But thou, when thou

prayest, enter into thine inner chamber, and having
shut thy door, pray to thy Father which is in secret,
and thy Father which seeth in secret shall recompense
thee."

The same principle of seeking only divine
praise is here applied to our approach to
God.   It seems to require no further notice, but we may consider here a subordinate principle which is applied also to
almsgiving and fasting—the principle of
recompense—"they have their reward."
Every kind of conduct gets its reward
on the plane of its motive.   If you look
out for human praise, on the whole you
get it.   If you aim vigorously at getting
on and winning a good position, the
chances are you will succeed.   On the
whole, then, you get the reward on
the plane of your motive.   And our Lord
recognizes these lower motives and their
proper reward ; and you find that in the
Old Testament, in many passages, God
is represented as being, as it were, careful
to distribute rewards on the lower plane.
See, for instance, how (in Ezek. xxix.
18–20) God notes that Nebuchadnezzar's
army served against Tyre and got no
wages ;   therefore He will give Egypt
for their wages,

So then if your motive is earthly, your reward is earthly. You "have out" your reward to the full, and must not imagine there is anything over and above which still appeals to God. When John Henry Newman was made a Cardinal, he—a devout, religious man, one of those who apparently without vanity have the power of talking about their own state of feeling—said he trembled to take this great honour, lest he should be taking out his reward here on earth; because he could not think that anything he had tried to do in his life was such that it would not have its reward exhausted by his receiving so great a position.

We need not scrutinize such an expression of fear too closely, but only notice that a real Christian, instead of being anxious to obtain recognition, is on the other hand rather alarmed if he always seems to get full credit for all that he tries to do. He believes that he is aiming only at the approval of God, and finds too liberal a reward in this world even disquieting, as though it were a sign that he was mistaken as to his motive.

Fasting

"Moreover when ye fast, be not, as the hypocrites, of a sad countenance : for they disfigure [1] their faces, that they may be seen of men to fast. Verily I say unto you, They have received their reward. But thou, when thou fastest, anoint thy head, and wash thy face ; that thou be not seen of men to fast, but of thy Father which is in secret : and thy Father which seeth in secret, shall recompense thee."

Here, under the head of fasting, we may notice again—what applies equally to prayer or almsgiving—that our Lord is passing no slight on " common " or public religious actions. St. Paul tells us (1 Cor. xvi. 2) that we are to have church collections ; and our Lord (St. Matt. xviii. 19–20) tells us we are to pray together ; and He instituted the Eucharist, which is the Church's chief social or public act of communion with God and mutual fellowship. So that it is ridiculous to suppose that our Lord is here slighting social religious acts— acts which are performed by the Church as a body, and in the performance of which we have the encouragement which comes of co-operation and the sense of

---

[1] " Disfigure " or possibly "conceal " their faces, so that by a form of dress drawn over the face they may be shown to be persons going about as penitents.

responsibility to the community as well as to God. And most of all it is ridiculous to suppose that our Lord is discouraging common fasts, but not common prayer or almsgiving. In no case is our Lord undervaluing the common religious acts. But He is indicating the new motive of religious action, whether it be prayer or almsgiving or fasting. Its motive is to be God, and not man.

Once more, our Lord is not here saying anything against the manifestation of our religion by outward acts. We cannot pray properly—speaking generally—without adopting a fit attitude in prayer, that is on the regular occasions of public and private prayer. We should pray in an attitude which befits our relation to God, on our knees, humbly, devoutly, because we are creatures of soul and body, and we cannot express the religious feeling of the soul properly without its influencing the gesture of the body also. We are made up of soul and body, and a " spiritual " act of worship is one in which the spirit, that is the will, heart, and intelligence is engaged ; not one in which the body takes no part. Then if we learn to pray aright, kneeling upon our knees,

5*

we can carry the habit of prayer into our common life. In the same way, if we are to fast, the act must have a definite and methodical outward expression. Do not let us be afraid of outward expressions of religion. Our Lord is emphasizing this, and this only, namely, the motive which we should have in all kinds of righteousness, whether it be worship or charity or self-subdual.

Thirdly, we shall do well to consider, what is the principle and meaning of fasting. Our Lord says less about it in the New Testament than about prayer ; and you notice in the Revised Version that the mention of it has vanished from a good many of those passages where in the Authorized Version it stood side by side with prayer.[1] It is quite true, then, to say that our Lord says less about fasting than about prayer. It is quite true that fasting may be abused, and was in our Lord's time abused, more easily than prayer ; but it is a great mistake, because you have got a certain truth, therefore to exaggerate it. Our Lord Himself fasted, as He prayed ; He fasted forty days and forty nights. Our Lord

[1] e.g. St. Matt. xvii. 21 ; St. Mark ix. 29 ; 1 Cor. vii. 5.

said the disciples should fast ; that it
would betoken the time when He was
taken from them.   St. Paul mentions
fasting as part of his own practice—" in
fastings often," and he bids Christians
" distress " [1] their bodies in order to
reduce them to subjection.   So again the
Church from the first has fasted.   And
the great authors of religious revivals in
our own Church—Simeon, and Pusey,
and Maurice alike—practised and encouraged fasting.   We may then depend
upon it that we are foolish if we neglect
it.   And the object of it is this : it is
the bringing the body under the spirit,
whereas without it the body is apt to
have the upper hand.   It is not because
our body is evil that we are to fast ; but
because our body is, or is meant to be,
holy, and the effective instrument of the
spirit.   People sometimes talk about their
body as if it were merely animal, and the
spirit were only attached to it.   That is
not true.   Our whole being is meant to be
spiritual, as governed by the spirit.   Just
as when the principle of life takes hold
on the inorganic world, it makes the
whole nature organic of living ; so when

[1] 1 Cor. ix. 27 ; 2 Cor. xi. 27.

the spirit takes hold of the animal body, its work is to make the whole body spiritual.

It is worth while dwelling on this. People often justify sensual sin by saying it is " natural ; " and the fallacy in this excuse lies in supposing that our body can be treated apart from our spirit. Nothing is natural to man in which his spiritual nature is not brought into play. This is the reason why Christian marriage is truly natural. It gives to the bodily relation of the sexes a spiritual purpose, and makes it serve high ends of the home and family. Thus in the same way eating and drinking is to serve spiritual ends. Everything that the true Christian does is part of a great spiritual whole ; and it is, I say, because our body has grown lawless, and is apt to trample upon the spirit instead of being subordinate to it, that we have, as it were, to take revenges on the body and from time to time to harass it, as St. Paul says, and to hold it as a slave.

For the same reason we are foolish and un-Christian if we fast in such a way, either excessively or unwisely, as to unfit the body for spiritual activities. If you fast so that you cannot work, you are violating your duty. But many people eat and drink and sleep too well; their bodies have the upper hand; and they ought to fast, and to take the opportunity of Lent to fast, that their bodies may be brought under their spirits.

> " The Scriptures bid us fast; the Church says, now :
> Give to thy Mother what thou wouldst allow
>   To ev'ry corporation."

Now we must return to consider the parenthesis about prayer which is to be found in chapter vi. 7–15, and which teaches us something more than that its motive is to be not vainglory, but God.

First, we are taught that prayer is not to be measured by length, but intensity :

> " And in praying use not vain repetitions, as the Gentiles do : for they think that they shall be heard for their much speaking."

If you were to go into a Buddhist country at the present time, you would find prayer there reduced to something so formal and mechanical that people do not need to say it themselves, but have prayer wheels and prayer flags to wind or spread out their prayers before the holy one. And I am afraid there has been a good deal of a like mechanical praying in the Christian Church. But the value of prayer, our Lord warns us, is not to be measured by its length, but the amount of will and intention we put into it. There is always need that we should remember this. There is always a danger that in praying dutifully and according to some rule our praying should be becoming mechanical, and that we should find ourselves measuring its value by its length.

Secondly, Christian prayer is not for the sake of informing God :

"Be not therefore like unto them [the Gentiles]: for your Father knoweth what things ye have need of, before ye ask him."

Why is it, then, that God requires of us to pray ? The answer is a quite simple one. It is because God is our Father, and He wishes us to be trained in habits of conscious intercourse with Him. Therefore, just as many blessings which God wishes to give us are made dependent on our working for them, so many other blessings are made dependent on our regular and systematic asking. God wills to give them, but He wills to give them only if we ask Him ; and this in order that the very necessity of continually holding intercourse with a personal God and making requests to Him may train us in the habit of realizing that we are sons of our heavenly Father. The wisdom of this provision is best realized if we reflect how easily, when the practice of prayer is abandoned, the sense of a personal relation to God fades out of our human life. We are to pray then not to inform God, but to train ourselves in habits of personal intercourse with our Father who is in heaven.

CHAPTER VII

THE LORD'S PRAYER

OUR Lord is not satisfied with giving us abstract principles of prayer, but teaches us how to pray by giving us an example :

"After this manner therefore pray ye : Our Father which art in heaven," &c.

In regard to this great prayer, I would content myself with calling attention to the points of chief importance, and trying to explain some few difficulties, which lie in the separate clauses, and then very briefly indicating some of the principles which as a whole it enshrines.

"Our Father which art in heaven."

The spirit of a prayer depends in great measure on whether the worshipper's thought of God is true or false, adequate or inadequate. The Christian invokes God under the completest of all His titles, the title of Father, for " God hath sent forth the Spirit of His Son into our hearts crying, Abba, Father." [1] And we call Him the *Father which is in heaven*, not because He is far off us—for in the Kingdom of Christ heavenly and earthly things are mingled and we " are come unto the heavenly Jerusalem," [2]—but because He is raised far above all the pollution and wilfulness and ignorance of man " as the heaven is higher than the earth." So we invoke our Father, infinitely above us yet unspeakably near. And the first prayer we offer is :

" Hallowed be thy name."

What is the name of God ? That is very well worth our consideration. The name of God in the Bible means that whereby He discloses or reveals Himself. You may indeed almost say that the name of God means God Himself as He is manifested. God has shown Himself to man ; He has spelt out His great name, letter by letter, syllable by syllable, before the eyes of men or into their hearts, in nature, in conscience, by the voice of His prophets and in Jesus Christ His Son. Thus to hallow or sanctify

---

[1] Gal. iv. 6.   [2] Hebr. xii. 22.

His name is to set store by His revelation
of Himself, as Father, Son and Spirit,
one God. To pray that His name may
be hallowed, is to pray that His revelation
of Himself may be accepted of men,
and His religion professed openly and
secretly : that He may be acknowledged
in conduct and worship, in Church and
in State, on Sunday and on week-day.

"Thy kingdom come."

The kingdom of God meant to the
Jews, of course, the kingdom of the
Messiah : that is to say that coming
age, when heaven and earth shall be
fused in one, when God shall be manifested in His glory, when all things
shall be seen in their true light, and
the reign of Christ in truth and meekness
and righteousness shall be not only real
but also manifest and indisputable. This
is " the end of the world," the " far
off, divine event," which is still future.
At times, indeed, the Church as it already
exists among us is called " the kingdom
of God," but at other times (as is implied
here) the Church is regarded as a divine
institution, representing indeed the kingdom here and now in the world, but

also preparing for its arrival in the future. To pray for the coming of the kingdom is therefore to pray for the spread and progress of the Church, and also for the diffusion in every way of all truth and meekness and righteousness and of all that can find its place in the city of God. It is to pray for the over- throw of every form of " lawlessness " —lawless lusts and appetites, lawless am- bition and insolence and denial, godless worldliness and lies and vanities, cruelty, oppression and malice in every shape. For all these are forms of rebellion ; and we know that they represent only a temporary usurpation. We are looking forward to, and would fain hasten, the coming of the King.

" Thy will be done, as in heaven, so on earth."

This is a prayer against all wilfulness and also against all sloth : a .prayer for the vigorous co-operation of all rational creatures in furthering the divine order of the world. And we should notice that the phrase " as in heaven, so on earth " refers probably to all the three preceding clauses : Hallowed be Thy Name, as in heaven, so on earth ; Thy kingdom

come, as in heaven, so on earth ; Thy
will be done, as in heaven, so on earth.
The Church of Rome, in the *Catechism*
put forth by the Council of Trent, specially
exhorts her clergy to call the attention
of the faithful to this connexion of the
clauses of the Lord's Prayer.

" Give us this day our daily bread."

Strangely enough, one of the most
difficult words in the whole New
Testament is this word translated "daily "
in the Lord's Prayer. Nobody can be
quite certain what it means, but probably
it means " the bread for the coming
day." [1] Give us to-day the bread for
the coming day, is therefore a prayer
that the bodily needs of the immediate
future may be supplied for all members
of the Christian family. It is a prayer
which only those can truly pray who
are contented with such satisfaction of
their bodily needs as enables them to
do the work of God, who will ask nothing
for themselves that they do not ask

[1] It is not improbable, as has been recently suggested
by Mr. Chase (see below, p. 135), that this expression,
occurring side by side with " this day," is due to the
use of the prayer both morning and evening. In the
morning Christians prayed " give us our bread to-day,"
and in the evening " give us our bread for to-morrow."

for others, and who are content to wait
from day to day upon the hand of God.

" And forgive us our debts, as we also have forgiven
our debtors."

We cannot do God's work without
the supply of our physical needs : therefore the last prayer was offered. But
equally we cannot do God's work unless
we are at peace with Him : therefore
this prayer follows. Sin may be regarded
from many points of view—as a flaw
or mistake in our nature or conduct :
as a violation or transgression of a divine
law (as in ver. 14) : or (as here) as an
act by which we have robbed God of
His rights and incurred an obligation or
debt which we cannot satisfy, and in
regard to which we can only appeal
to the divine pity. From the first point
of view what is needed is nothing else
than recovery and correction : from the
second point of view we need forgiveness,
but forgiveness of such sort as is only
morally possible when our will is brought
back into harmony with our Father's
will. Only from the third point of view
is forgiveness the same as being let off.
And the position which the petition to
be forgiven holds in this prayer, prevents

us from supposing that we can be " forgiven our debts " without having been
brought into union with God's will and
into the fellowship of His Kingdom.

On the principle involved in this
petition our Lord Himself immediately
comments :

" For if ye forgive men their trespasses, your
heavenly Father will also forgive you. But if ye
forgive not men their trespasses, neither will your
Father forgive your trespasses."

Here is the divine principle which, as
we noticed before, is made so plain in
the parable (St. Matt. xviii. 31), where
the unthankful servant finds that all the
debt which had been forgiven him has
rolled back upon him because he in his
turn has behaved himself unforgivingly,
unmercifully, towards his fellow-servant.
God deals with us as we deal with our
fellow-men ; and if we want to know
how the face of God looks towards us,
we must examine ourselves to see what
is the aspect we present towards them.

" And bring us not into temptation."

Now, this clause is intelligible enough
to our hearts, but rather difficult to
explain exactly. St. James writes, " My

brethren, count it all joy when ye fall into divers temptations." How can we pray not to be tempted or tried when we know that it is only through temptation that we can become strong ? One explanation is to be got from our Lord's words to His disciples at the time of His agony in the garden : " Watch and pray, that ye enter not into temptation." If you fail to be on your guard, if you live carelessly, without watching or praying, God suffers you, as a punishment, to be brought within the scope of temptation, and you find it too strong for you. Therefore the prayer may be interpreted by expansion thus : make us watchful and prayerful, so that we never be suffered to fall into temptation as into a snare. But it seems better to interpret the prayer more generally as the expression of that self-distrust for which we have only too sufficient grounds, as a prayer like that of Christ's, " Father, if it be possible let the cup of trial pass from me without my drinking it, nevertheless, thy will be done." [1]

[1] The difficulty experienced in regard to this clause by the early Christians is well known. I may refer to Mr. Chase's Lord's Prayer in the Early Church (Texts and Studies, Cambridge, 1891), pp. 60 ff. Mr. Chase

" But deliver us from the evil one."

That is " from the devil." Modern
society seems to be very unwilling to
believe in the devil or diabolical temptation. It has been cleverly said, " Satan
never did a more successful stroke than
when he persuaded people to disbelieve
in his own existence." There is truth
in that. It is a real hindrance to our
spiritual struggle, and an increase of
despondency, if we forget that evil solicita-
tions come, not only from our own
nature, but from evil spirits. Moreover,
if Christ is a true prophet—if He dis-
cerned the conditions of our spiritual
struggle—certainly diabolical temptation
must be real, for He is always talking of
it. When He sees evil at work, evil for
body or soul, His mind penetrates behind
the appearances and detects hostile wills

also points out the close resemblance between the
" Lord's Prayer " and our Lord's own language of
prayer or about prayer in the time of the passion.
" Father . . . Thy will be done. . . ." " Pray that ye
enter not into temptation." " I pray that thou shouldest
keep them from the evil one." There are other resemblances perceptible in the prayer recorded in St.
John xviii.

In the original language used by our Lord " Lead [us
not into temptation "] and " Enter [into temptation "]
would only be different forms of the same verb.

working to pervert the kingdom of God, hostile wills which He knows are to be at last subdued to God and are even now controlled by Him, but which He knows also to be at present active and malevolent. He looks forth upon the disorder of the world and says, " An enemy hath done this."   And He teaches us to pray for deliverance from the evil one.

The familiar doxology " For Thine is the kingdom, the power and the glory, for ever and ever, Amen," which in our Church, though not over the greater part of Christendom, follows here, was not in the original Lord's Prayer, though it was added to it very early. It was a doxology in use in the early Church, which was added at the end of many of the prayers, and which in very early times came to be attached to the Lord's Prayer in some of the manuscripts. It was thus given a place which it cannot rightly claim, though it states, grandly enough, the reason why we thankfully worship the Father.

It remains for us to notice some of the great principles which are enshrined in the Lord's Prayer as a whole.

1. The Lord's Prayer is not one prayer among many, as you may have a number of collects for a number of different objects, and each particular collect is just one prayer among many. The Lord's Prayer is rather the type and mould of all Christian prayer : " After this manner pray ye." Understand the Lord's Prayer, and you understand altogether how to pray as a Christian should. It is not really an exaggeration to say that the climax of Christian growth is to have thoroughly learned to say the Lord's Prayer in the spirit of Him who first spoke it.

And this has been clearly recognized in the use which the Church in all ages has made of the Lord's Prayer. Among human compositions there are hardly any more beautiful than the liturgies in which Christians, at the altar, have approached the Father of their Lord in the pleading of His sacrifice. Now, almost all the ancient liturgies, both Eastern and Western, are so constructed that the point upon which each service converges is the saying of the Lord's Prayer. That is the point up to which they climb. That is their central act ; because

the highest thing in the way of worship
that the Christian can do is to say Christ's
own prayer in the freedom of that approach to God once won for him by the
Son of Man.

So, in our English Communion service,
we put ourselves into the right frame
of mind by saying the first Lord's Prayer ;
and afterwards, in the power of His
sacrifice and in the unity of His life
communicated to us in His body and
blood, we say again the Lord's Prayer
with its doxology as the highest point
of our whole service.

Once more, in the daily offices of morning
and evening prayer the Lord's Prayer
occurs at the beginning, and again in
the prayers after the Creed. It occurs
at the beginning to put us into the
right frame of mind for praying ; and at
the end it sums up our petitions—all
that we have learned to pray for in
the Psalms and lessons. And to leave
out the second Lord's Prayer, as is
sometimes done by way of shortening
the service, is surely to betray ignorance
of the structure of the service and of the
use of the Lord's Prayer.

This is indeed the way in which the

Church, catching the spirit of her Lord,
has used the Lord's Prayer ; and, as
individuals, it is a great happiness and
power for us when we have learned to
use it freely. Whatever particular object
we may want to pray for, we have never
prayed for it aright till we have prayed
for it in the words and spirit of the
Lord's Prayer. That, I repeat, is not
one prayer among many. It covers all
legitimate Christian praying, and indeed
the saying of it affords the best test
whether our wants of the moment can
become a prayer offered " in the name
of Christ."

2. I say " in the name of Christ." The
Lord's Prayer is the great prayer in His
name. You know how many people have
a very strangely childish notion, that
praying in the name of Christ means
simply the addition of the words " through
Jesus Christ our Lord " at the end of
their prayers. But depend upon it they
do not by adding these words, or any
words, bring it about that their prayers
should be in the name of Christ. To
pray in the name of Christ means to pray
in such a way as represents Christ. The
representative always must speak in the

spirit and meaning of those for whom he speaks. If Christ is our representative, that must be because He speaks our wishes, or what we ought to make our wishes; and if we are to pray in the name of Christ, that means that we are, however far off, expressing His wishes and intentions.

Therefore, as this Lord's Prayer represents profoundly and perfectly the spirit of Him who first spoke it, and who taught it to His Church, it follows that it is, beyond all other prayers, the prayer in Christ's name. Do you then want to know whether this or that thing can be prayed for in Christ's name ? The answer is to be found in another question, Can it be legitimately covered by the clauses of the Lord's Prayer ?

3. The knowing and saying of the Lord's Prayer, as the prayer in Christ's name, was in the early Church regarded as being, like the knowing and saying of the Creed, the privilege of those only who were members of the Christian family. It was the prayer of the family because of its first words, " Our Father." The Christian creed, we know, would teach us to believe that God is the father of all

men, and that He wills all men to realize their sonship. They cannot reach true manhood till they have come to know themselves to be, and to realize what is involved in being, sons of God.

But since sin has separated men from God, it is through Christ and by the partaking of His Spirit that they enter or re-enter into the privileges of sonship. Thus the right of calling upon God as " Our Father " was believed to have come with the coming of the gift of the Holy Ghost : " God has sent forth the Spirit of His Son into our hearts, whereby we cry, Abba, Father." We are apt to have rather " free and easy " notions of the divine fatherhood. And it is important to be reminded that to call God our Father, we must ourselves be sons, and it is they who are led by the Spirit, they and they only, that are the sons of God.

This Lord's Prayer then is the prayer of the great Christian family ; the prayer of the whole Catholic Church ; the prayer which, though it may be spoken by a single member in a quiet corner, yet is instinct with the aspirations and needs and wants of all that great society which represents all nations and kindreds and peoples and tongues in this world and in that which lies beyond the grave.

4. There is a searching lesson which lies in the order of the petitions in the Lord's Prayer; for in praying much depends on the order in which we rank the objects of prayer.

There is a saying, not recorded in our canonical Gospels, but which yet the very earliest traditions of the Church treasured, and ascribed to our Lord; the saying is this: " Ask for great things, and the small things will be given unto you. Ask for heavenly things, and the earthly things will be given unto you." Now, that is exactly the spirit of the Lord's Prayer. It puts our wants in the right order. It puts first the heavenly things, the great things, and not the little things, the earthly things, the things that seem to touch us closest.

We know that it is not easy to adopt this order in our prayers. There are many who have lost altogether the habit of praying and who are won back to it by some anxiety or trouble that touches them nearly. Some son or daughter perhaps lies dying, and the father and mother, who long have been alien to the habit of prayer, are driven back to it by the very stress of their pressing need. Or some calamity is threatening to over-whelm ourselves, and we fall on our knees, after a great interval of prayerlessness, to implore that it may be averted. And, of course, we must bless God that anyhow men should be brought to pray : and God can lead us to higher things through things which touch our flesh and blood, from earth to heaven. But the point is that that is not the right order of prayer. The true Christian does not pray first for the things that most nearly touch himself. That impulsive prayer which springs simply out of our own needs is not the prayer " in the name of Christ."

We remember what our Lord said to the disciples in those solemn hours in the upper chamber before His passion : " Hitherto ye have asked nothing in my name." They had presented all kinds of petitions and requests ; but in their own name. So it is so often with us. Hither-to have we asked nothing in His name. But that of course is a fault to be altered. We must let our prayers be in Christ's name : that is to say in the order reflected in the Lord's Prayer.

Now, let us examine it. The prayer of human instinct runs : My Father, give me to-day what I so sorely require. But the Lord's Prayer begins with " Our Father "—not " my," but " our." I must begin with losing my selfishness, with recollecting that I am only one of the great body of God's children, of the great mass of humanity. Thus I cannot ask for anything for myself which conflicts with the interests of others. And the invocation proceeds, "which art in heaven." It places us in a reverent way at the feet of God. " God is in heaven, and thou upon earth : therefore, let thy words be few."

" Hallowed be Thy name." It puts God's revelation of Himself to men above all human needs. We are so apt to think last of the glory and honour of God ; but here as we pray we are forced to exalt it into the first place ; and next, " Thy kingdom come." That is—May that divine order which, point by point, in many parts and many manners, through all the great web of history, has gradually to be woven out—may that great purpose of God find at last its fulfilment. Thus we are forced as we pray to merge our

6

own narrow interests and schemes till they are lost in the largeness and wisdom of the divine method.

" Thy will be done on earth as it is in heaven." Here we are forced to bend our stubborn or short-sighted wills to conformity with the divine will and to make the law of heaven the pattern for earth. Only then, when we have exalted God's glory above man's need, when we have subordinated our little designs utterly to the great purpose of God, when we have bent our little wills under the great and divine will—only then are we allowed to express our wants for ourselves.

And even so how modestly, how restrictedly. " Give us," we pray, not anything that we may want, but " to-day the bread for to-morrow : " enough to do God's work upon in God's way ; and so that our eating may not involve others' hungering. And then, because we cannot do God's work unless we are in His peace, " Forgive us our trespasses "—not anyhow ; but according to that necessary law by which God deals with us as we deal with others ; " as we forgive them that trespass against us." And, because we are weak and frail, " lead us not into temptation, but deliver us from the evil one."

Is there not then in this prayer the whole philosophy of praying ? And when we come to think of it, we shall find that the philosophy or secret of prayer lies in the recognition of the same law of correspondence, which has been the secret of scientific progress in the development of the resources of nature, and which, in that department, Francis Bacon has the credit of teaching men, or of putting into words for them. Before his time men had been trying to get extraordinary good things out of nature in accordance with the whims and fancies of astrologers and alchemists : they had dreamt of making gold, or finding the elixir of life. But all this was profitless because it was done in ignorance of nature's actual laws. And Bacon spoke a prophetic word when he said " Nature can only be controlled by being obeyed ; " that is — in reverent correspondence with nature as it is, is the secret of power. Now, in the higher region, that is what our Lord taught us about prayer. Man had been offering all sorts of prayers, sacrifices, propitiations. That God mercifully regarded such ignorant worship we cannot doubt : but it *was* ignorant of God's character and method. Now, so far as is good for us, our Lord has enlightened us about the nature and method of God : and He has shown us that prayer should not be an attempt to impose our own whims and fancies on the wisdom of God, but a constant act of correspondence by which we bring our short-sighted wills and reasons into corre- spondence, the intelligent correspondence of sons, with the perfect reason and will of God, the all-wise Father of all human souls and of the great universe.

5. Here finally we find an answer to all our manifold questionings as to what we may pray for, and what we may not.

Our Lord gave us that answer also in another way at another time—in the prayers of His passion. In His passion He prayed for the coming of the kingdom, in that great prayer recorded in St. John's Gospel. He prayed then without quali- fication. Similarly, He prayed for those rough soldiers who were unwittingly doing Him such awful wrong : " Father, forgive them, for they know not what they do." But when, in the garden, He asked to be Himself delivered from the coming agony, in the true humility of His manhood He prayed conditionally, " Father, *if it be possible*, let this cup pass from me."

Now, that is exactly the lesson of the Lord's Prayer. There are many things which God has revealed to us that He intends to give us. He has promised that He will give us all those things which belong to His kingdom and its righteousness. For these things we can pray, not only urgently, but with the certainty of faith that we must win them for ourselves and others by importunate asking. We cannot, of course, force the will of others, but we can with the assurance of faith win for others, as for ourselves, the spiritual opportunities, resources, and advantages of God's kingdom.

There are also many things God has revealed that He does not mean to give us, and there are laws of His ordering, spiritual and physical, that by revelation or natural investigation He has made known. For these things, then, or against these laws, we must not pray ; we must not ask that God will violate His general laws in our private interest.

But there is a great mass of things which lie in between these two regions of certainty. We do not know if it is God's will that this or that person should recover from sickness, or this or that calamity should be averted. God is wiser than we are. We do not know whether it is God's will that we should have the rain that is so necessary for our crops. There are things like these that lie in a region of uncertainty into which the intelligence of man cannot penetrate. So then as the object of prayer is not to bring the divine will down to the human, but to lift the human up into correspondence with the divine, for all these uncertain things we can pray indeed, but uncertainly—" If it be possible, let this or that come to pass ; nevertheless, not my will, but Thine, be done."

CHAPTER VIII

UNWORLDLINESS

THE keynote of St. Matthew vi. is, as we have seen, this : that the true motive of the religious life in all its activities is simply the desire for divine approval. It owns one only master, God, whom it trusts with an absolute confidence. There results from this a complete freedom from the anxieties of the world. It is then an unworldly disposition, as the result of simplicity of motive, that our Lord proceeds to enjoin :

" Lay not up for yourselves treasures upon the earth, where moth and rust doth consume, and where thieves dig through and steal : but lay up for yourselves treasures in heaven, where neither moth nor rust doth consume, and where thieves do not break through nor steal : for where thy treasure is, there will thy heart be also."

In the days when our Lord spoke these words people mostly preserved their money and other treasures by concealing it, as in many parts of Europe they do still. Thus

the task of thieves was, in the main, to
" dig through " into places in houses or
fields where treasure was likely to be
hidden. This is the meaning of our
Lord's metaphor. We are to lay up our
store in heaven, where no thief can get
at it, and where no natural process of
corruption can affect it. Now heaven
is God's throne. It is where His will
works centrally and peacefully ; and the
kingdom of the Christ is the kingdom of
heaven, because, though a visible society
in the world, God is there specially known
and recognized, and His good will towards man is consequently at work with
a special freedom and fullness.

If then you are asked, what is it to lay
up treasure in heaven, I think you may
answer with great security : To lay up
treasure in heaven is to do acts which
promote, or belong to, the kingdom of
God ; and what our Lord assures us of is
that any act of our hands, any thought
of our heart, any word of our lips, which
promotes the divine kingdom by the
ordering whether of our own life or of
the world outside—all such activity,
though it may seem for the moment to
be lost, is really stored up in the divine

treasure-house ; and when the heavenly
city, the New Jerusalem, shall at last
appear, that honest effort of ours, which
seemed so ineffectual, shall be found to
be a brick built into that eternal and
celestial fabric.

And our Lord gives the answer to a
difficulty continually perplexing honest
Christians—How am I to learn to *love*
God ?   I want to do my duty, but I do not
feel as if I loved God. Our Lord gives
the answer, " Where your treasure is,
there will your heart be also." Act for
God : do and say the things that He
wills : direct your thoughts and intentions
God-ward ; and depend upon it, in the
slow process of nature all that belongs
to you—your instincts, your intelligence,
your affections, your feelings—will gradually follow along the line of your action.
Act for God : you are already *showing*
love to Him and you will learn to *feel* it.

" The lamp of the body is the eye : if therefore
thine eye be single, thy whole body shall be full of
light. But if thine eye be evil, thy whole body
shall be full of darkness. If therefore the light
that is in thee be darkness how great is the darkness !
No man can serve two masters : for either he will
hate the one, and love the other ; or else he will
hold to one, and despise the other. Ye cannot
serve God and mammon."

6*

The question of vital importance is therefore simply this : are we single-minded in seeking God ? Single-mindedness is what gives clearness and force to life. Put God clearly and simply first in great things and in small. Then your life will be full of light, full of power. And, in fact, you must put God first, or nowhere. Examine any man's life, of what sort it is. Cross-question it. You will find at last that one motive is dominant. Either, at the last push, he will do God's will, or he will do that by which he thinks to serve his interests in the world. Now, what a man does at the last analysis or when pushed into a corner, that is what reveals his real motive. The motive on which he then acts is his only real master-principle. There can be only one such in a life. At the bottom it is either God which rules a life or mammon, i.e. money. Thus you must put God first, or, in fact, you are putting Him nowhere ; if He is not first, then He can be no more than the superficial decoration of a life really devoted to something else.

But how can it be, we ask, that the exclusive service of God in all things will not narrow our life ? How can God be so

" jealous " without restricting our legitimate freedom of expansion ? For this
reason : that God contains everything in
Himself, the whole sum of being ; so that
there is no beauty or truth or goodness in
the world which does not fall to you to
delight in as part of your love and service
of God. Loving God and serving Him
should lead you to watch for and respond
to all the truth and beauty that there is
in God's world, all the traits of excellence
in human character, and to own your
allegiance to your family, to your friends,
to your country, to your Church, and to
humanity as a whole. " All things are
yours, whether Paul, or Apollos, or Cephas,
or the world, or life, or death, or things
present, or things to come ; all are yours,"
if " ye are Christ's," as " Christ is God's." [1]

Never let us fear then that to put God
first and serve Him utterly will narrow
any faculty or dwarf any capacity. It can
but fill with an evergrowing largeness
every vital force of our being, every instinct of our life. " If thine eye be single,
thy whole body shall be full of light."

But we must notice the warning which
our Lord gives us as to a possible condition

[1] 1 Cor. iii. 22, 23.

of our conscience. The light that is in us
may be darkness. We so often talk as
if we were only obliged to " follow our
conscience : " as if no one could lay anything to our charge unless we were acting
against the present voice of conscience.
But this is a very perilous error. We are
also obliged to enlighten our conscience
and to keep it enlightened. It is as much
liable to error as our uninstructed intelligence, as much liable to failure as our
sight. Probably of every ten criminals
brought up before judge and jury on
account of some crime the majority were
not, at the time of its commission, acting
against their conscience. They had stifled
or darkened that long ago. There is, I
believe, nothing to which in our time
attention needs to be called more than
to the fact that conscience is only a
faculty for knowing God and His will. It
is certain, unless it is educated, to give
wrong information. And the way to
educate it, is to put it to school with the
" Light of the world." Alas ! there must
be multitudes of respectable and self-
enlightened people of whom it is true
that the light which is in them is darkness.

The result of singleness of mind in seeking God is to be a complete freedom from worldly anxiety. The keynote, as it were, of the passage which concludes this chapter is the phrase, " Seek ye first the kingdom of God and His righteousness, and all the rest shall be added unto you." Look to God first. Obey God. Enthrone Him in unique supremacy in your heart. He is your Father, and as such you can trust Him. If day by day you do His will simply, and cast your care on Him, then you can have a wonderful freedom from anxiety as to your future, and can live at peace—the sort of peace which finds its illustration in the fascinating tranquillity of the flowers of the field, and the light-heartedness of the birds of the air. These are our Lord's words :

"Therefore I say unto you, Be not anxious for your life, what ye shall eat, or what ye shall drink ; nor yet for your body, what ye shall put on. Is not the life more than the food, and the body than the raiment ? Behold the birds of the heaven, that they sow not, neither do they reap, nor gather into barns ; and your heavenly Father feedeth them. Are not ye of much more value than they ? And which of you by being anxious can add one cubit unto his stature ? And why are ye anxious concerning raiment ? Consider the lilies of the field, how they grow ; they toil not, neither do they spin : yet I say unto you, that even Solomon in all his glory was not arrayed like one of these. But if God doth so clothe the grass of the field, which to-day is, and to-morrow is cast into the oven, shall he not much more clothe you, O ye of little faith ? Be not therefore anxious, saying, What shall we eat ? or, What shall we drink ? or, Wherewithal shall we be clothed ? For after all these things do the Gentiles seek ; for your heavenly Father knoweth that ye have need of all these things. But seek ye first his kingdom, and his righteousness ; and all these things shall be added unto you. Be not therefore anxious for the morrow : for the morrow will be anxious for itself. Sufficient unto the day is the evil thereof."

Anxiety—that is what we are to be freed from. It is not forethought, or " carefulness " in that sense, against which our Lord is warning us, but anxiety. We are to trust God. To do daily the duty of the day, and then trust God for the consequences.

Our pattern in this freedom from anxiety is, of course, our Lord Himself. You notice that through all His ministry He looked forward, and lived His life as a whole, on a certain plan ; but there was no anxiety as to results. It is a sort of symbol of this attitude of mind that once, amidst the howling storm on the lake, the Master was found asleep on a pillow. It is, as it were, an object lesson of what is said in Psalm cxxvii ; which more than

anything in the Old Testament expresses
our Lord's meaning in this passage :

" It is vain for you that ye rise up early, and so
      late take rest,
   And eat the bread of toil :
   For so he giveth unto his beloved sleep."

That is the motto to write under the
picture of Christ in the boat on the stormy
sea.

Our Lord here, as elsewhere, is manifestly expressing Himself in the proverbial
manner. It is the proverbial manner to
express a thing by an extreme one-sided
instance. We have noticed this repeatedly:
and that, for this reason, one proverbial
utterance may need to be balanced by
another contrary one. Thus, on another
occasion our Lord bids us take thought
of what His service will involve, looking
towards the future like a man who is
about to build a house or a king who
is preparing for a campaign. Here He is
putting the other thought, that we are to
cast all our care upon God our Father,
who careth on our behalf.

But indeed if taking this passage alone
you think of the metaphors which our
Lord employs—metaphors of the flowers

of the field and the birds of the air—you
will see that what He means to warn us
against is anxiety, not prevision. For think
of the growth of the plant; it is always
looking towards the future in its own
instinctive way; the process by which
it grows is a gradual process; all its
activity is directed towards the preparation of the seeds by which the permanence
of the species is secured. And so with
the birds when they build their nests:
they are making provision. Everything
is done by bird and plant in view of the
future, but done with a tranquillity which
reposes unconsciously upon the purpose
of God. What they do unconsciously
we are to do consciously.

Here, then, is a lesson specially necessary for our time. There is no greater
plague of our generation than the nervous
anxiety which characterizes all its efforts.
How many people are there who make
their health much worse than it would
naturally be, because they are always
morbidly anxious about their symptoms
or some possibility of infection. Again
and again it is anxiety about health which
is a main cause of our unserviceableness
in doing our duty. We ought to be reason-

ably careful and to go boldly forward in the peace of God.

Again, how many good schemes fail because people are so nervously anxious about their success that they never reach that condition of peaceful persistence in work which is necessary if it is to be fruitful. " Semper agens, semper quietus " —" always at work, always tranquil "— that is the right motto.

Once more, as to holidays. What a vast mistake people often make in turning a holiday into an occasion of solicitude ; seeking for distraction at the expense of repose, and forgetting that the only central repose for wearied or jaded faculties is the reposing upon the Eternal. There alone is " the central peace subsisting at the heart of endless agitation." People would get much more even of physical good from Sunday and holiday rests, if they used them first of all as occasions for returning to God and finding rest in Him. And this applies to the clergy no less than to the laity. " Be still, then, and know that I am God." That is what we are to learn. Repose upon God quietly, and do daily the duties of the day, and bear daily the evils of the day, and, like Christ our

Lord, though it be through cross and passion, we shall come to the glory which is predestined for us by God.

And observe the phrase, " Sufficient unto the day is the *evil* thereof." Our Lord is not in any sort of way promising us that we shall not suffer trouble if we put our trust in God. What He tells us is simply that " According to thy day, so shall thy strength be." We are in God's hands. God gives us the evil and the good. We are only, like our Lord, to trust in His divine fatherhood ; and doing our best to-day, exercising our judgement to the best of our power, we are to repose in His love.

CHAPTER IX

CHRISTIAN CHARACTERISTICS

THE seventh chapter—the last which belongs to the Sermon—is occupied with a number of accessory topics. The character of the citizen of the kingdom of God has now been portrayed for us ; the relation of this character to the old law has been explained ; its main motive or principle has been described. Now there follow some characteristics which flow naturally from the relation in which the citizen of the kingdom stands both towards God and towards man. The first of these is the uncritical temper. " Judge not and ye shall not be judged."

THE UNCRITICAL TEMPER

We should observe that in the parallel passage in St. Luke vi. this exhortation follows very suggestively upon a description of the character of God which corresponds to an earlier passage in St.

Matthew's account of the Sermon on the Mount. " Ye shall be the sons of the Most High ; for he is kind toward the unthankful and the evil. Be ye merciful, even as your Father is merciful. And judge not," &c. That is to say, God is not critical ; He does the best for every one. He gives to every one the gifts he can appreciate. This is to be embodied in the temper of the disciple.

" Judge not, that ye be not judged. For with what judgement ye judge, ye shall be judged ; and with what measure ye mete, it shall be measured unto you. And why beholdest thou the mote that is in thy brother's eye, but considerest not the beam that is in thine own eye ? Or how wilt thou say to thy brother, Let me cast out the mote out of thine eye ; and lo, the beam is in thine own eye ? Thou hypocrite, cast out first the beam out of thine own eye ; and then shalt thou see clearly to cast out the mote out of thy brother's eye."

Manifestly, what is in our Lord's mind is the temper and character of the Pharisee. The Pharisee was in his way a strict religionist, a strict observer of religion. But you may almost say that the Pharisee tested progress in religion by the capacity to condemn other people. " This multitude which knoweth not the law is accursed." [1] The Pharisee had

[1] St. John vii. 49.

passed through a certain probation in learning. He had, as it were, passed his examinations and stood his tests; and now he was in a position to set every one else in his proper and subordinate place. That was the very test of his progress, that he was able to " despise others "; and it followed that he could be, in regard to his own *inner* character, lax and self-satisfied. He had attained the right standard; he was performing the right observances. So long as he did these things, he need not be over-scrupulous in examining himself. Therefore the Pharisee was both critical and hypocritical; critical with regard to others, with regard to himself hypocritical.

Our Lord, then, did not mean to make of His disciples a new kind of Pharisee. He did not mean that His disciples, as they grew to learn and follow the strictness of their Master's standard, should come to be supercilious like the Pharisees, and, like them, morally hollow. Therefore He warns against these two easily combined characteristics.

On the contrary, the temper which our Lord approves is the humility which

makes the best of others, and is severe
with itself. You, He seems to say, have
every opportunity to know your own
failings ; therefore look stringently to
yourself, " the mote, or the beam, that
is in thine own eye." That " bulks big "
enough in your own vision. To consider
it prevents you from over-estimating
yourself, and humbles you in your own
sight. Let it also take out of your
heart and off your lips all the readiness
to criticize and condemn other people.

Make the best of others. For that
is, in fact, what our Lord means by
" judge not." It is what we should
most naturally express by " Do not be
critical." Because a thing is strange or
new to you, because it does not fall
in with your ideas, do not condemn it
off-hand, but try to appreciate it with
sympathy first of all. Make the best of
every thing and every person. And there
is no doubt that if after looking for
the good points in any idea, or undertaking, or person, you are at last bound
to condemn, the weight attaching to
your adverse verdict will depend very
largely on whether you have escaped
the reputation of being a " critical "

and censorious person. The condemna-
tion of one who is always finding fault
carries no moral weight.

I say, If at last you are bound to
condemn, and that may be the Christian's
duty. For here, again, as throughout
this Sermon, we must notice our Lord's
proverbial method, otherwise we may
misinterpret altogether the temper which
our Lord here commends. There is a
temper of universal toleration very pre-
valent in our age, both in conversation
and in literature ; which can indeed
tolerate everything, because it has no
fixed standards of right and wrong, of
true and false, at all. But it is clear
enough that this was not what our
Lord meant to recommend ; it would be
so utterly antagonistic to His own character. No one is severer in discriminating
judgement than our Lord when the occasion requires it. More than this, our
Lord did deliberately intend that His
Church, and the members of His Church,
should have standards of goodness and
truth which should enable them—aye,
which should require them when duty
called—to condemn their own brethren.
A passage in St. Matthew's Gospel which

has been referred to already is clear upon this. " If thy brother trespass against thee "—are you to say, " It is of no account. It is not my business to condemn ? " No. When it is not a question of the love of criticizing or of uncharitable judgement, but of maintaining the law of right and wrong, then it becomes our business to judge, and after consideration and patience to condemn.

" Go, shew him his fault between thee and him alone ; if he hear thee, thou hast gained thy brother. But if he hear thee not, take with thee one or two more, that at the mouth of two witnesses or three every word may be established. And if he refuse to hear them, tell it unto the church : and if he refuse to hear the church also, let him be unto thee as the Gentile and the publican. Verily I say unto you, What things soever ye shall bind on earth shall be bound in heaven ; and what things soever ye shall loose on earth shall be loosed in heaven." [1]

Our Lord does here actually commit to the Church—as on an earlier occasion to St. Peter as the chief and representative apostle—not the right, but the duty, to bind and to loose : that is, to pass judgements as to what is right and what is wrong, what is to be permitted and what is not to be permitted, in the

[1] St. Matt. xviii. 15–18.

Christian society. Again, after His resurrection He gives to His apostles the power and the duty to apply these judgements to persons, to absolve and to retain sins.[1] Thus the Church, and each of its members, is not indeed to be censorious in temper, or to make the worst of people; but, when occasion requires, is to maintain the moral standard. So it is that St. Paul expressly tells the Corinthian Church that, as a Christian society, they are to judge, not those that are without, but those that are within their own body: and he severely condemns them because they had let pass, or tolerated, a serious moral offence without discriminating judgement being passed upon it.[2]

It is the same where doctrine is concerned. The New Testament continually warns Christians that they are to have standards of judgement; to test all things, and hold fast that which is right;[3] to test the spirits whether they be of God.[4] And if any teacher come with a doctrine calculated to subvert the principles which lie at the basis of the

---

[1] St. John xx. 23. [2] 1 Cor. v.
[3] 1 Thess. v. 21. [4] 1 John iv. 1.

Christian life, St. Paul and St. John
alike recommend an attitude towards
him which cannot exactly be described
as tolerance.

> "As we have said before, so say I now again, If
> any man preacheth unto you any gospel other than
> that which ye received, let him be anathema."
> "If any one cometh unto you, and bringeth not
> this teaching, receive him not into your house, and
> give him no greeting : for he that giveth him greeting
> partaketh in his evil works." [1]

These injunctions are given in view of
cases where fundamental matters of principle are at stake. About minor matters
St. Paul adopts a tone of the widest
toleration.[2]

There is then a duty of judgement :
while on the other hand our Lord condemns the critical and censorious temper.
Is it not true that a candid conscience
finds very little difficulty in distinguishing
the duty of judgement from the sin of
censoriousness and criticism ? And is it
not the case that those who have the
lowest and vaguest standards of what is
true and right, are yet very often the most
critical in judgement of other people ?

We are then to be anxious to make
the best of others : and our Lord here

[1] Gal. i. 9 ; 2 John 10–11.   [2] Rom. viii. 14.

again recognizes that law which we have so
often heard from His lips, that God deals
with us as we deal with our fellow-men.

" Judge not, that ye be not judged. For with
what judgement ye judge, ye shall be judged : and
with what measure ye mete, it shall be measured
unto you."

This describes no doubt how God will
deal with us. And from the parallel
passage of St. Luke we should gather
that the retaliation will not be confined
to God. As we deal with other men, so
other men also will deal with us.

" And judge not, and ye shall not be judged : and
condemn not, and ye shall not be condemned : release,
and ye shall be released : give, and it shall be given
unto you ; good measure, pressed down, shaken
together, running over, shall they give into your
bosom. For with what measure ye mete, it shall be
measured to you again." [1]

From all sides you get as you give. If
you deal with men in the critical, censorious, narrow temper, men will deal so
with you. If you make the best of others,
others will make the best of you.

RESERVE IN COMMUNICATING RELIGIOUS
PRIVILEGES

The next characteristic of the temper

[1] St. Luke vi. 37–38.

of the Christian follows by way of contrast
on what has gone before. It is reserve
in communicating religious privileges.

" Give not that which is holy unto the dogs, neither
cast your pearls before the swine, lest haply they
trample them under their feet, and turn and rend
you."

There are high privileges which many
men cannot appreciate ; and if you
press these upon them, you must not
be surprised if, indignant with you for
having given them something which seems
so worthless, they take violent reprisals
upon you.

We ask the question, Has our Lord,
in inculcating the uncritical temper,
inculcated the undiscriminating temper
also ? Certainly not. That which the
Christian has received is of inestimable
worth. The kingdom of God, as our
Lord told us, is like a pcarl of great
price, which when a man hath found,
for joy thereof he goeth and selleth all
that he hath and buyeth that pearl.
The Christian knows what it is to be
a Christian, admitted into the fellowship
of God, illuminated by His truth, em-
powered by His Spirit. In the light of
God in which he lives he cannot but

gaze out into the world with a dis-
crimination like his Lord's.

Our Lord, we notice, gave men the
best they were capable of receiving.   To
all the world, if they had but the faith
to trust His power, He gave the out-
pouring of that power in works of healing.
He had compassion on them ; He gave
them what alone they were capable of
appreciating—kindness, goodness.   But
did He teach all men the highest truth ?
No.   He sifted, He discriminated them,
till He had got those to deal with who
really had ears to hear the highest truth,
and then He told it them.   Our Lord
did not cast His pearls before swine,
lest they should turn again and rend Him.

Thus we are to put before men what
they are capable of appreciating.   Not
by any merits of ours, God has given
us admission to His fellowship ; He has
given us great things and small things.
We are not to be selfish misers, we are
to be anxious to communicate all ; but
we are to be discriminating.   Kindness,
self-sacrifice, care for their interests, and
their whole life—that all men can appreciate, and we are to give it to all.
But we are not to shriek the highest

truths of religion at the street corner. We are to wait till people show a desire for the deepest things before we offer them religion. There is to be reserve in communicating religious privileges and religious truths.

Such was the method of the early Church. It went out into the world. It let all the world see the beauty of its life, the glory of its brotherhood, the splendour of its liberality. It made men feel that Christians were the friends of God. But it did not teach them the secrets of its life—its Creed, its Eucharist, its Prayer—till they were ready for them, and showed their readiness at least by inquiry. The Church would explain herself in apologies and dissipate misconceptions, but it was not her way to press her innermost truths upon the indifferent.

At the same time the Church has not an esoteric system, like the Pagan mysteries, or the schools of Gnosticism. These Gnostics would have only the intellectual admitted to the mysteries of God. That was not the Church's way ; her way was to teach *every* man (who would come with faith), that she might present every man perfectly initiated in Jesus Christ.[1] The Church believed that nothing was necessary for the highest union with God but a simple sense of sin and faith in God, in His Son, in His Spirit. Nothing was necessary but these qualities of wanting and trusting, which are possible to all men. Her cry was—" Ho ! every one that thirsteth, come ye to the waters." Only, let them come thirsty !

And surely that method which belonged to the early Church—although no doubt it was capable of being abused—is yet the true and best method. Let the Church show her compassion and goodness and geniality to all men, but not press upon them the mysteries of God until, under her discipline and teaching, they begin to show some disposition to receive them. This is a principle which admits of very different applications in a heathen country, in preaching religion among nominal Christians, and in the social intercourse of individuals ; but it admits of some application everywhere. And above all let us take care that the Church appears before men's eyes as offering provision of spiritual privileges not for

[1] Col. i. 28.

those who can pay for them, but for those who have some measure of spiritual appetite.

Impartial Considerateness

The Christain is to be discriminating, but not niggardly. On the contrary, recognizing the readiness of God to give in response to human prayer and effort, he will exhibit a like impartial benevolence towards all men. This is the last of the three characteristics of the Christian character which our Lord enjoins : impartial benevolence proceeding from its own experience and knowledge of the divine character.

" Ask, and it shall be given you ; seek, and ye shall find ; knock, and it shall be opened unto you : for every one that asketh receiveth ; and he that seeketh findeth ; and to him that knocketh it shall be opened. Or what man is there of you, who, if his son shall ask him for a loaf, will give him a stone ; or if he shall ask for a fish, will give him a serpent ? If ye then, being evil, know how to give good gifts unto your children, how much more shall your Father which is in heaven give good things to them that ask him ? All things therefore whatsoever ye would that men should do unto you, even so do ye also unto them : for this is the law and the prophets."

As reported by St. Luke, our Lord gives a commentary on " Knock, and it shall be opened unto you." For He gives us the parable of one who comes at an inconveniently late hour, and knocks at the door of a neighbour's house, and demands food for a friend who has unexpectedly arrived. And our Lord represents how the owner of the house is at last unwillingly overcome by the importunity of the applicant, and consents to rise and give his neighbour what he wants.

Our Lord then in His proverbial way lays down the general principle that importunity—asking, seeking, knocking—at last overcomes all obstacles and obtains what it wants. And we notice that our Lord first arouses attention by the indiscriminate assertion of this general principle. Having done that, when the attention of men was arrested, He on different occasions—for those who had ears to hear—modified it, or gave it its more definite meaning.

Such modifications or exacter definitions are the following : " All things whatsoever ye pray and ask for, *believe that ye have received them and ye shall have them* " (St. Mark xi. 24). " *If ye abide in me, and my words abide in you,* ask whatsoever ye will, and it shall be

7

done unto you " (St. John xv. 7). ' Hither-
to have ye asked nothing *in my name* :
ask, and ye shall receive " (St. John xvi.
24). It is not too much to say that all
these three statements are in effect identical. To ask in Christ's name is to ask
in accordance with Christ's will, and this
brings the third statement into identity
with the second. We can only, as intelligent sons of our Father, " believe that
we have received " requests which we
know to be in accordance with His mind.
Thus the first statement, in common
with the other two, makes the effective
prayer the prayer which rises in intelligent
correspondence with the revealed will and
character of God.

Even in this passage may be found a
suggestion to the same purpose. " What
man is there of you," asks our Lord,
" who, when his son asks a loaf or a fish,
will give him "—something that looks
like what he has asked for, but is in fact
wholly useless or noxious ? If then
human fathers are to be relied upon in
this way, much more is our heavenly
Father to be relied upon to give good
things to them that ask Him. But there
is a converse to that statement. If a

son asks for something harmful, what will a wise father do ? Not give him what he asks for, but give him according to his request as it is interpreted by his own larger wisdom. So it is with God. He must hear and answer prayers, not simply as they are ignorantly offered, but as interpreted for our good in accordance with His wise purposes. Roman Catholics and Anglicans and Eastern Christians and Nonconformists may be praying for unity among Christians, each according to their own preconceptions. God will be attentive to the good-will of their prayers : they will not, as has been suggested, " neutralize one another : " for God will answer them according to His own wisdom.

Very suggestive then is the version of this saying of our Lord which is given by St. Luke : " Shall not your Father which is in heaven give "—not good things, but— " the Holy Spirit to them that ask Him ? "

It is often said, we know, that the Sermon on the Mount contains no dogmas, no doctrines. But it implies, in a remarkable way, two cardinal Christian doctrines : the Godhead of Christ and the " fallen " state of man. The Godhead of

Christ, as has been and will again be noticed, is involved in the authoritative tone in which He speaks. And a significant expression in this paragraph is unintelligible unless all men, even the best, may be assumed to be sinful. For our Lord is talking about good parents who will do their best for their children : yet He says " If ye, *being evil.*" Now, I do not know any words which could more forcibly imply—all the more forcibly because incidentally, or by the way—that our Lord thought of us all as having something evil and corrupt in our nature as it is ; so that every one of us needs regeneration and conversion, in order that we may become what our Lord would have us. The intimation seems to me to be indeed the more emphatic because, as I say, it is uttered by the way. " If ye, being evil, know how to give good gifts unto your children, how much more . . ."

Finally, on these considerations of the divine goodness, our Lord bases our duty towards our fellow-men.

" Therefore whatsoever ye would that men should do unto you, even so do ye also unto them : for this is the law and the prophets."

Our conduct towards our fellow-men is to be the reflection of that benevolence which we have learned and experienced in our own relations to God.

In the maxim in which our Lord expresses our social duty there are several points which require notice.

(1) In its negative form it had been already announced both among the Jews and among the Greeks :   ' Do not do unto others what you would not have them do unto yourselves." [1]   But one great superiority of our Lord over other teachers lies in the positive character of His teachings. His will is not simply that men should abstain from wrong-doing, but rather that they should be occupied in right-doing.

(2) Here, as elsewhere, our Lord is proverbial ; and this maxim must not be interpreted " at the foot of the letter." Nothing in common life is more annoying than when people do so interpret and act upon it ; with the result that they behave as if every one must agree with them in

[1] The reference is to the saying of Hillel, " What to thyself is hateful, to thy neighbour thou shalt not do ; this is the whole law and the rest is commentary " (cp. *Tobit* iv. 15 ; *Did.* i. 3), and to the similar maxim suggested by Plato and current among the Stoics.

what they like or dislike. What is meant of course is that we are to act towards others with the same considerateness which we would desire that others should exhibit towards us.

(3) We must realize that here we have the very kernel of Christian social duty. There was a great truth announced by the philosopher Immanuel Kant: " So act as to treat humanity, whether in thine own person or in that of any other, in every case as an end withal, never as a means only." We are to treat all men always as ends in themselves ; never as means merely towards some other end which we have in view, whether it be production, or convenience, or pleasure. Now this is only putting into a philosophical form what our Lord states more simply, more practically. We are to take the same thought for others that we would have others take for ourselves. We are to make no exceptions in our own favour. We are to love our neighbour as ourselves. We are to remember that every one in God's sight counts for one ; and that nobody counts for more than one. This, I say, is the principle of all Christian social conduct. It is the principle of

justice ; that is, of equal consideration. We could go on drawing out its applications for hours, and never have exhausted them. And it cannot be said that it is at present within reasonable distance of being realized in what is called Christian society. We have a more or less true ideal of what our own human life ought to be—of what opportunities we ought to have for the development of our faculties—of what home and school and college, youth and married life and old age, work and rest, ought to mean for ourselves and our families. We are to make these ideals universal. We are so to limit our desires that what we want for ourselves we can reasonably expect also for others. We are to be as truly zealous and active for other classes or other individuals as we are for our own class or our own family or ourselves. The service which we expect from others, we are to see that we render in some real sense to them, and that without respect of persons. This maxim is not inconsistent with inequality of position or (within limits) of wealth—for men are differently constituted in their capacities and wants—but it does demand equality of consideration.

(4) " This," our Lord says, " is the law and the prophets," that is, this is the principle in which the true spirit of the Old Testament culminates. There was, of course, much in the Old Testament narrower than this and on a lower level ; and, as we have seen, our Lord occupied a large part of this sermon in showing us those points in which the Christian law is to supersede the legislation of the Old Testament. But the Old Testament represents throughout a process of growth ; and this is the point towards which it tends and in which it culminates. As St. Paul says, " If there be any other commandment it is briefly comprehended " —summed up, or accomplished—" in this saying, namely, Thou shalt love thy neighbour as thyself." [1]

[1] Rom. xiii. 9.

CHAPTER X

FINAL WARNINGS

OUR Lord concludes the Sermon on the Mount with three emphatic and striking warnings. We may paraphrase them thus:—There are two ways in life, the easy way of self-pleasing and the hard way of self-denial. Many are found to seek the first, few to tread the second. But they lead directly away from one another: and the first is the way to death, the second is the way to life.

There are many voices of teachers in the world, speaking fair-sounding words. But not by their words, nor by the results they seem to win, shall men be judged by the Son of Man, but by their characters.

There are many spiritual fabrics which men are raising. They seem the one very much as good as the other; but the test lies in their capacity to last. And no spiritual fabric that is built on anything else than the teaching of the Son of Man can endure the strain and stress which will come upon it before the end.

Let us direct our attention to each of these three warnings in turn.

THE TWO WAYS

" Enter ye in by the narrow gate : for wide is the gate, and broad is the way, that leadeth to destruction, and many be they that enter in thereby. For narrow is the gate, and straitened the way, that leadeth unto life, and few be they that find it."

This is the " doctrine of the two ways." Human instinct has seized on the metaphor in many parts of the world ; the easy way of self-pleasing, the difficult way of duty. It speaks home to every heart, to every intelligence, and nothing needs to be said about it.   But I would ask your attention to one question which in our time arises instantly as we read these words—Are we to suppose that our Lord is here saying that at the last issue many will be " lost " and few " saved " ?   Is this the meaning of " Few be they that find it " ?

To this question we may reply thus : On one occasion the disciples categorically asked our Lord, " Are there few that are being saved ? "   and our Lord replied,

" Strive to enter in by the narrow door."
And on another occasion Peter asked the
question about John, " What shall this
man do ? " and was answered, " What
is that to thee ? Follow thou Me." [1]
Beyond all question, our Lord does not
intend us to know the answer to the
questions which our curiosity raises as
to the ultimate destinies of men. He
fixes our attention, we may say, on three
great principles : the character of God
our Father, and His impartial, individual,
disciplinary love : the final and universal
victory of His kingdom over all resisting
forces within and without : the critical
character of our present life with its
capacities for good or for evil, and the
limitless consequences for good or evil
which flow from the present attitude of
each individual towards his personal responsibilities.

It is not unfair to translate our Lord's
words here, " Many there be that *are
entering* the broad way ; few there be
that *are finding* the narrow way." Thus
they embody what is always found to be
true in the experience of men. Always,
to one who wants to do his duty, it

[1] St. Luke xiii. 23-49 ; St. John xxi. 21-22.

will become plain in the long run that
he has to be prepared to stand alone, or
at any rate to go against the majority.
He cannot tell the opportunities and
responsibilities that others may have.
He knows that God is infinitely con-
siderate, and will do the best possible
for every soul that He has created ;
but he can, he does, know his own responsibility and his own duty, and in
following that he will have to bear the
burden of going with the few and watching
the spectacle, so depressing or staggering
to the imagination, of the multitude
running to do evil.

CHARACTER THE ONE THING NEEDFUL

" Beware of false prophets, which come to you in
sheep's clothing, but inwardly are ravening wolves.
By their fruits ye shall know them. Do men gather
grapes of thorns, or figs of thistles ? Even so every
good tree bringeth forth good fruit ; but the corrupt
tree bringeth forth evil fruit. A good tree cannot
bring forth evil fruit, neither can a corrupt tree
bring forth good fruit. Every tree that bringeth
not forth good fruit is hewn down, and cast into
the fire. Therefore by their fruits ye shall know
them. Not every one that saith unto me, Lord,
Lord, shall enter into the kingdom of heaven ; but
he that doeth the will of my Father which is in
heaven. Many will say to me in that day, Lord,
Lord, did we not prophesy by thy name, and by
thy name cast out devils, and by thy name do many

mighty works ? And then will I profess unto them,
I never knew you : depart from me, ye that work
iniquity."

There is nothing against which our
Lord warns us so terribly as against
hypocrisy. The discernment of French-
men and Germans has detected, or fancies
it has detected that Englishmen are
specially liable to be hypocrites, to profess
what they do not practise, to care for
the outward appearance of morality and
religion while they neglect their inward
essence. Whether this be specially true
of us or no, it behoves us to look to
ourselves. In literature, in journalism,
in the pulpits, in political life, there are
so many " prophets," so many professors,
so many remedy-mongers. They speak
fair words, and brilliant success often
seems to attend them. " Have we not
prophesied in Thy name," they cry, " and
in Thy name cast out devils, and in
Thy name done many wonderful works ? "
But not all the fair-seeming words, not
all the brilliant, even miraculous successes,
can compensate for the absence of personal
character. That is the one thing to
which our Lord looks. He warns us
that not the most brilliant results can

avail anything if we lack that inner character which is like Christ's.

This is a tremendous warning for days of wide and somewhat vague philanthropy, of restless activity, of nervous anxiety for successes and results, for days such as our own day. It is a tremendous warning for days of journalism, when every one is tempted to advertise himself or allow himself to be advertised, when everything is dragged prematurely into publicity, and even those who are working for Christ are apt to be morbidly anxious to produce results which can be tabulated in parish magazines or even proclaimed in newspapers. We need to remember that all these results in Christ's eyes will not bear looking at, except so far as they are the product of inward Christian character, a character which He can recognize as His own. For He cannot accept anything, whatever its orthodox profession, in which He does not trace the lineaments of His own character.

There are two other points which may be overlooked in this paragraph but which are of great importance. First, our Lord does encourage us or even

command us to believe that wherever
there is the good character, the Christlike
character, there the Holy Spirit is at
work. God works far beyond His own
appointed channels. The principle of
loyalty and obedience binds us who know
His will to use His sacraments, His instituted ordinances; but God is not
tied to His own ordinances. He can
work wherever He sees the good disposition; and it is blasphemy against
His Spirit to deny that He is at work
anywhere where we witness the forming
of the Christian character. The good
fruit cannot come from anything else
than the good tree.

Then, secondly, we should notice the
claim which our Lord here makes for
Himself. Without preface, without em-
phasis, as a matter of course, He implies
that He is the final judge of all men,
not only as to the outward results they
achieve, but also as regards the secret
inner motives of their hearts and the
character of their lives. " Many shall
come to me in that day," i.e. in " the
Day of Jehovah," the day of final assess-
ment—" They will come to *Me*; they
will profess loyalty to *Me*, saying, ' Lord,

Lord '; they will plead their good works :
but I shall discern the true inner character of their lives." Many Jews of our
Lord's day in Palestine believed that
the Son of Man, the Messiah, would act
as the vicegerent of God in "the day
of judgement," at "the end of the
world." In implying that He would so
act our Lord is, in other words, professing
that He is the Messiah : but, more than
this, He gives to the Messianic claim a
depth and fullness of meaning which
makes it identical with a properly *divine*
claim. Can one conceive men living,
as the Apostles lived, with one who
they were led to believe was the ultimate
judge of their outward conduct and of
their secret thoughts, the ultimate arbiter
of their destinies, the final Justice, without
passing into an attitude towards Him
of awe, trust, and worship, which would
be idolatrous and disastrous if He to
whom it was directed was not truly
divine ?

Again, is it even conceivable that any
man could claim to be in this inner
introspective sense the final judge of all
men without being either (with reverence
be it spoken) a tremendous blasphemer

or the very Son of God, of the Father's own nature ?

ENDURANCE THE TEST

And lastly, our Lord gives the warning that each spiritual fabric must be judged by its power of lasting.

" Every one therefore which heareth these words of mine, and doeth them, shall be likened unto a wise man, which built his house upon the rock : and the rain descended, and the floods came, and the winds blew, and beat upon that house : and it fell not ; for it was founded upon the rock. And every one that heareth these words of mine, and doeth them not, shall be likened unto a foolish man, which built his house upon the sand : and the rain descended, and the floods came, and the winds blew, and smote upon that house ; and it fell : and great was the fall thereof."

Here, again, is the tremendous claim : the only solid foundation for life is Jesus and His words.

We know how this necessity of a rock-like foundation for a spiritual structure, and the possibility of finding such a foundation only in His own words and person, were illustrated by our Lord's method in the foundation of His Church. A crowd came round Him at the first, offering Him the same kind of allegiance which men will give to spiritual teachers

and benefactors in moments of enthusiasm. " Many believed on his name,
beholding the signs which he did." And
our Lord stood strangely aloof from them.
" He did not trust himself unto them,"
St. John says, " for that he knew all
men, and because he needed not that
any should bear witness concerning man,
for he knew of himself what was in
man." [1]   So He tested the would-be
disciples, till at last by His strange
self-withdrawing ways, by His severe
words, by His enigmatic utterances, He
had sifted out those who were really
in earnest in following Him from those
who were not; exhibiting in all this
a strange contempt for majorities or
mere numbers. At last He had gathered
round Him the little band of those
who were really ready to follow and
obey to the uttermost, the band of His
apostles. Here were men who had indeed
got down to the rock, and were building
on it and nothing short of it. Here
were men who could trust Him and His
word, and take as the basis for their
life the confession of His name. Therefore, like that on which they built, they

[1] St. John ii. 23–25.

were themselves rock-like, and not as
the shifting sand of ordinary human
nature. These then could be used as
the foundations of Christ's new society.
So under circumstances where a special
strain was put upon their loyalty, He
asked the great question of the apostles ;
and Peter gave the great answer : " Thou
art the Christ, the Son of the living
God." Then, as it were with a sigh of
relief, our Lord turns upon him, and
greets him with His supreme benediction,
and recognizes in him—if not yet something which is ready to His hand, yet
something which is capable of being
made ready :

"Blessed art thou, Simon Bar-Jonah : for flesh
and blood hath not revealed it unto thee, but my
Father which is in heaven. And I also say unto
thee, that thou art Peter—rock-man—and upon
this rock I will build my church." [1]

Thus our Lord illustrated in His own
practice what He teaches here. He would
have men dig down to the rock, and
build their spiritual fabrics there ; and
the rock is nothing else than His own
person and His own word. To hear
Him, and go away without imbibing

[1] St. Matt. xvi. 17.

His teaching and putting it into practice, to be nominally a Christian but in reality of the world, that is to build a house upon the sand.

And the test of all spiritual fabrics is their capacity to stand the strain of wild and rough experiences. That is a formidable lesson for an age of rapid workmanship; an age which resents the necessity for underground work and silent preparation.

It suggests a momentous question with regard to the spiritual fabric of our own personal lives, and also in regard to any spiritual enterprise in which we may be engaged: Have we dug deep enough and got down to the rock, or have we preferred quick results to solid foundations? Have we thought Christ's words impossible of application, and so been content with something short of Him? If so, our work is doomed. It will not last. It will not stand the rain and the wind and the storm.

We see how true this principle has proved in the history of the Church of Christ, which was built on the solid rock of His word and person. The Catholic Church through all vicissitudes has

yet endured. Body after body naming
the name of Christ have arisen and
seemed to succeed better than the Church
for a time, generally through some defect
in her teaching or character : for it
has been generally through the fault
of the Church that they have arisen,
and on the neglect of the Church's duty
that they have spread. But these bodies
have not exhibited lasting power. Any
great catastrophe which, as it were,
shatters the structure of human society
down to its foundations, brings to naught
multitudes of enterprises which seemed
successful. But there is one society which
has exhibited a marked capacity for
lasting, which after whatever vicissitudes
has shown that it has still the power of
recovery and persistence. This is that
Church which is rooted on the word of
Christ, which has the succession from
His apostles, in which are administered
His sacraments according to His appoint-
ment, which holds to His apostolic tradition, and appeals back to His sacred
Scriptures.

That is the test—to last ! We must
apply it to our own lives. We know
that temptation is both thorough and

searching, and that our moral and religious
principles will in different ways be tested
to the uttermost. To stand the test
and carry our moral being through it
all to victory—that is the one thing
that matters ; and to make this possible
there is one sovereign expedient—that
is thorough and whole-hearted conversion
of our will, our intellect, our affection,
to Christ and His word.

"And it came to pass, when Jesus ended these
words, the multitudes were astonished at his teaching:
for he taught them as one having authority, and
not as their scribes."

And here we leave the great sermon.
It is not, as some suppose, the whole
of Christianity. Those who have been
inclined so to esteem it have been apt
to underrate the amount of theological
doctrine which is to be found in it. It
postulates, as we have seen, two central
doctrines : that of the divinity of Christ's
person, and that of the sinfulness of
human nature. But, even so, it is not
the whole of Christianity. It begets in
us, or develops and deepens, the s nse
of sin, and so may be said to point to
what it does not teach, the atonement
by which our Lord has expiated the

sins of the world, and brought us back
to reconciliation with our Father which
is in heaven. But again an atonement
which merely secured our forgiveness for
past sins would be no real remedy. It
would leave us weak as we were before.
Nothing can satisfy us but actual and
permanent redemption from the power
and the taint of sin. Thus again the
sermon may be said to point forward to
that great supply of moral power which
by the coming of the Spirit of God has
been given inwardly in the hearts of His
people. It is that inward grant of Christ-
like power—the administration of the
Spirit—which is the real essence of Christianity. All else is a preparation for it.
Christianity is not so much a statement
of the true end or ideal of human life
as it is a great spiritual instrument for
realizing the end.

The realizing of the moral end of life
—that is the test of your Christianity.
Be sure of that. The hold we have
on our creeds, the use we make of the
sacraments, can be judged by one test—
do they lead to the formation in us of
Christian character ? The character may
be cleansed and perfected after death,

but here and now is our opportunity for laying its foundations deep and firm, and showing its power to absorb the whole of our being. That is the test which we cannot press home upon ourselves too often—am I becoming like Christ ? Many will come to Him in that day with a record of their orthodoxy and of their observances, of their brilliant successes in His professed service ; but He will protest unto them, " I never knew you." He " knows " no man in whom He cannot recognize His own likeness.

APPENDICES

APPENDIX I

THE SERMON ON THE MOUNT

AND seeing the multitudes, he went up into the mountain : and when he had sat down, his disciples came unto him : and he opened his mouth and taught them, saying,

Blessed are the poor in spirit : for theirs is the kingdom of heaven.

Blessed are they that mourn : for they shall be comforted.

Blessed are the meek : for they shall inherit the earth.

Blessed are they that hunger and thirst after righteousness : for they shall be filled.

Blessed are the merciful : for they shall obtain mercy.

Blessed are the pure in heart : for they shall see God.

Blessed are the peacemakers : for they shall be called sons of God.

Blessed are they that have been persecuted for righteousness' sake : for theirs is the kingdom of heaven. Blessed are ye when men shall reproach you, and persecute you, and say all manner of evil against you falsely, for my sake. Rejoice, and be exceeding glad : for great is your reward in heaven : for so persecuted they the prophets which were before you.

Ye are the salt of the earth : but if the salt have lost its savour, wherewith shall it be salted ? it is thenceforth good for nothing, but to be cast out and

PARALLEL PASSAGES FROM ST. LUKE.[1]

St. Luke vi. 20–49.

And he lifted up his eyes on his disciples, and said, Blessed are ye poor : for yours is the kingdom of God. Blessed are ye that hunger now : for ye shall be filled. Blessed are ye that weep now : for ye shall laugh. Blessed are ye, when men shall hate you, and when they shall separate you from their company, and reproach you, and cast out your name as evil, for the Son of man's sake. Rejoice in that day, and leap for joy : for behold, your reward is great in heaven : for in the same manner did their fathers unto the prophets. But woe unto you that are rich ! for ye have received your consolation. Woe unto you, ye that are full now ! for ye shall hunger. Woe unto you, ye that laugh now ! for ye shall mourn and weep. Woe unto you, when all men shall speak well of you ! for in the same manner did their fathers to the false prophets.

xiv. 34, 35.

Salt therefore is good : but if even the salt have lost its savour, wherewith shall it be seasoned ? It is fit neither for the land nor for the dunghill : men cast it out. He that hath ears to hear, let him hear.

[1] Those not occurring continuously in chap. vi. are printed in italics.

trodden under foot of men. Ye are the light of the world. A city set on a hill cannot be hid. Neither do men light a lamp, and put it under the bushel, but on the stand ; and it shineth unto all that are in the house. Even so let your light shine before men, that they may see your good works, and glorify your Father which is in heaven.

Think not that I came to destroy the law or the prophets : I came not to destroy, but to fulfil. For verily I say unto you, Till heaven and earth pass away, one jot or one tittle shall in no wise pass away from the law, till all things be accomplished. Whosoever therefore shall break one of these least commandments, and shall teach men so, shall be called least in the kingdom of heaven : but whosoever shall do and teach them, he shall be called great in the kingdom of heaven. For I say unto you, that except your righteousness shall exceed the righteousness of the scribes and Pharisees, ye shall in no wise enter into the kingdom of heaven.

Ye have heard that it was said to them of old time, Thou shalt not kill ; and whosoever shall kill shall be in danger of the judgement : but I say unto you, that every one who is angry with his brother shall be in danger of the judgement ; and whosoever shall say to his brother, Raca, shall be in danger of the council ; and whosoever shall say, Thou fool, shall be in danger of the hell of fire. If therefore thou art offering thy gift at the altar, and there rememberest that thy brother hath aught against thee, leave there thy gift before the altar, and go thy way, first be reconciled to thy brother, and then come and offer thy gift. Agree with thine adversary quickly, whiles thou art with him in the way ; lest haply the adversary deliver thee to the judge, and the judge deliver thee to the officer, and thou be cast into prison. Verily I say unto thee, Thou shalt by no means come out thence, till thou have paid the last farthing.

St. Luke xi. 33.

No man, when he hath lighted a lamp, putteth it in a cellar, neither under the bushel, but on the stand, that they which enter it may see the light.

xvi. 17.

But it is easier for heaven and earth to pass away, than for one tittle of the law to fall.

xii. 58, 59.

For as thou art going with thine adversary before the magistrate, on the way give diligence to be quit of him ; lest haply he hale thee unto the judge, and the judge shall deliver thee to the officer, and the officer shall cast thee into prison. I say unto thee, Thou shalt by no means come out thence, till thou have paid the very last mite.

Ye have heard that it was said, Thou shalt not commit adultery : but I say unto you, that every one that looketh on a woman to lust after her hath committed adultery with her already in his heart. And if thy right eye causeth thee to stumble, pluck it out, and cast it from thee : for it is profitable for thee that one of thy members should perish, and not thy whole body be cast into hell. And if thy right hand causeth thee to stumble, cut it off, and cast it from thee : for it is profitable for thee that one of thy members should perish, and not thy whole body go into hell. It was said also, Whosoever shall put away his wife, let him give her a writing of divorcement : but I say unto you, that every one that putteth away his wife, saving for the cause of fornication, maketh her an adulteress : and whosoever shall marry her when she is put away committeth adultery.

Again, ye have heard that it was said to them of old time, Thou shalt not forswear thyself, but shalt perform unto the Lord thine oaths : but I say unto you, Swear not at all ; neither by the heaven, for it is the throne of God ; nor by the earth, for it is the footstool of his feet ; nor by Jerusalem, for it is the city of the great King. Neither shalt thou swear by thy head, for thou canst not make one hair white or black. But let your speech be, Yea, yea ; Nay, nay : and whatsoever is more than these is of the evil one.

Ye have heard that it was said, An eye for an eye, and a tooth for a tooth : but I say unto you, Resist not him that is evil : but whosoever smiteth thee on thy right cheek, turn to him the other also. And if any man would go to law with thee, and take away thy coat, let him have thy cloke also. And whosoever shall compel thee to go one mile, go with him twain. Give to him that asketh thee, and from him that would borrow of thee turn not thou away.

Ye have heard that it was said, Thou shalt love thy neighbour, and hate thine enemy : but I say

St. Mark ix. 43–48.

And if thy hand cause thee to stumble, cut it off : it is good for thee to enter into life maimed, rather than having thy two hands to go into hell, into the unquenchable fire. And if thy foot cause thee to stumble, cut it off : it is good for thee to enter into life halt, rather than having thy two feet to be cast into hell. And if thine eye cause thee to stumble, cast it out : it is good for thee to enter into the kingdom of God with one eye, rather than having two eyes to be cast into hell ; where their worm dieth not, and the fire is not quenched.

St. Luke xvi. 18.

Every one that putteth away his wife, and marrieth another, committeth adultery : and he that marrieth one that is put away from a husband committeth adultery.

vi. 27–36.

But I say unto you which hear, Love your enemies, do good to them that hate you, bless them that

unto you, Love your enemies, and pray for them that persecute you ; that ye may be sons of your Father which is in heaven : for he maketh his sun to rise on the evil and the good, and sendeth rain on the just and the unjust. For if ye love them that love you, what reward have ye ? do not even the publicans the same ? And if ye salute your brethren only, what do ye more than others ? do not even the Gentiles the same ? Ye therefore shall be perfect, as your heavenly Father is perfect.

Take heed that ye do not your righteousness before men, to be seen of them : else ye have no reward with your Father which is in heaven.

When therefore thou doest alms, sound not a trumpet before thee, as the hypocrites do in the synagogues and in the streets, that they may have glory of men. Verily I say unto you, They have received their reward. But when thou doest alms, let not thy left hand know what thy right hand doeth : that thine alms may be in secret : and thy Father which seeth in secret shall recompense thee.

And when ye pray, ye shall not be as the hypo- crites : for they love to stand and pray in the syna- gogues and in the corners of the streets, that they may be seen of men. Verily I say unto you, They have received their reward. But thou, when thou prayest, enter into thine inner chamber, and having shut thy door, pray to thy Father which is in secret, and thy Father which seeth in secret shall recom- pense thee. And in praying use not vain repetitions, as the Gentiles do : for they think that they shall be heard for their much speaking. Be not therefore like unto them : for your Father knoweth what things ye have need of, before ye ask him. After this manner therefore pray ye : Our Father which art in heaven, Hallowed be thy name. Thy kingdom come. Thy will be done, as in heaven, so on earth. Give us this day our daily bread. And forgive us our debts, as we also have forgiven our debtors.

curse you, pray for them that despitefully use you.
To him that smiteth thee on the one cheek offer also
the other; and from him that taketh away thy
cloke withhold not thy coat also. Give to every one
that asketh thee; and of him that taketh away thy
goods ask them not again. And as ye would that
men should do to you, do ye also to them likewise.
And if ye love them that love you, what thank have
ye? for even sinners love those that love them.
And if ye do good to them that do good to you, what
thank have ye? for even sinners do the same. And
if ye lend to them of whom ye hope to receive, what
thank have ye? even sinners lend to sinners, to
receive again as much. But love your enemies, and
do them good, and lend, never despairing; and
your reward shall be great, and ye shall be sons of
the Most High: for he is kind toward the unthankful
and evil. Be ye merciful, even as your Father is
merciful.

St. Luke xi. 1–4.

*And it came to pass, as he was praying in a certain
place, that when he ceased, one of his disciples said unto
him, Lord, teach us to pray, even as John also taught
his disciples. And he said unto them, When ye pray
say, Father, Hallowed be thy name. Thy kingdom
come. Give us day by day our daily bread. And*

8

And bring us not into temptation, but deliver us from the evil one. For if ye forgive men their trespasses, your heavenly Father will also forgive you. But if ye forgive not men their trespasses, neither will your Father forgive your trespasses.

Moreover when ye fast, be not, as the hypocrites, of a sad countenance : for they disfigure their faces, that they may be seen of men to fast. Verily I say unto you, They have received their reward. But thou, when thou fastest, anoint thy head, and wash thy face ; that thou be not seen of men to fast, but of thy Father which is in secret : and thy Father, which seeth in secret, shall recompense thee.

Lay not up for yourselves treasures upon the earth, where moth and rust doth consume, and where thieves break through and steal : but lay up for yourselves treasures in heaven, where neither moth nor rust doth consume, and where thieves do not break through nor steal : for where thy treasure is, there will thy heart be also. The lamp of the body is the eye : if therefore thine eye be single, thy whole body shall be full of light. But if thine eye be evil, thy whole body shall be full of darkness. If therefore the light that is in thee be darkness, how great is the darkness ! No man can serve two masters : for either he will hate the one, and love the other ; or else he will hold to one, and despise the other. Ye cannot serve God and mammon. Therefore I say unto you, Be not anxious for your life, what ye shall eat, or what ye shall drink ; nor yet for your body, what ye shall put on. Is not the life more than the food, and the body than the raiment ? Behold the birds of the heaven, that they sow not, neither do they reap, nor gather into barns ; and your heavenly Father feedeth them. Are not ye of much more value than they ? And which of you by being anxious can add one cubit unto his stature ? And why are ye anxious concerning raiment ? Consider the lilies of the field, how they grow ; they toil *forgive us our sins ; for we ourselves also forgive every one that is indebted to us. And bring us not into temptation.*

St. Luke xi. 34–36.

The lamp of the body is thine eye : when thine eye is single, thy whole body also is full of light ; but when it is evil, thy body also is full of darkness. Look therefore whether the light that is in thee be not darkness. If therefore thy whole body be full of light, having no part dark, it shall be wholly full of light, as when the lamp with its bright shining doth give thee light.

xvi. 13.

No servant can serve two masters : for either he will hate the one, and love the other ; or else he will hold to one, and despise the other. Ye cannot serve God and mammon.

xii. 22–34.

Therefore I say unto you, Be not anxious for your life, what ye shall eat ; nor yet for your body, what ye shall put on. For the life is more than the food, and the body than the raiment. Consider the ravens, that they sow not, neither reap ; which have no store-chamber nor barn ; and God feedeth them : of how much more value are ye than the birds ! And which of you by being anxious can add a cubit unto his stature ? If then ye are not able to do even that which is least, why are ye anxious concerning the rest ? Consider the lilies, how they grow : they toil not, neither do they spin ; yet I say unto you, Even Solomon in all his glory was not arrayed like one of these. But if God doth so clothe the grass in the field, which to-day is, and to-morrow is cast into the oven ; how much more shall he clothe you, O ye of little faith ? And seek not ye what ye shall eat, and what ye shall drink, neither be ye of doubtful

not, neither do they spin : yet I say unto you, that
even Solomon in all his glory was not arrayed like one
of these. But if God doth so clothe the grass of the
field, which to-day is, and to-morrow is cast into the
oven, shall he not much more clothe you, O ye of
little faith ? Be not therefore anxious, saying,
What shall we eat ? or, What shall we drink ? or,
Wherewithal shall we be clothed ? For after all
these things do the Gentiles seek ; for your heavenly
Father knoweth that ye have need of all these things.
But seek ye first his kingdom, and his righteousness ;
and all these things shall be added unto you. Be
not therefore anxious for the morrow : for the
morrow will be anxious for itself. Sufficient unto
the day is the evil thereof.

Judge not, that ye be not judged. For with what
judgement ye judge, ye shall be judged : and with
what measure ye mete, it shall be measured unto
you. And why beholdest thou the mote that is in
thy brother's eye, but considerest not the beam that
is in thine own eye ? Or how wilt thou say to thy
brother, Let me cast out the mote out of thine eye ;
and lo, the beam is in thine own eye ? Thou hypocrite, cast out first the beam out of thine own eye ;
and then shalt thou see clearly to cast out the mote
out of thy brother's eye.

Give not that which is holy unto the dogs, neither
cast your pearls before the swine, lest haply they
trample them under their feet, and turn and rend
you.

Ask, and it shall be given you ; seek, and ye shall
find ; knock, and it shall be opened unto you : for
every one that asketh receiveth ; and he that seeketh
findeth ; and to him that knocketh it shall be opened.
Or what man is there of you, who, if his son shall
ask him for a loaf, will give him a stone ; or if he
shall ask for a fish, will give him a serpent ? If ye
then, being evil, know how to give good gifts unto
your children, how much more shall your Father

*mind. For all these things do the nations of the world
seek after : but your Father knoweth that ye have need
of these things. Howbeit seek ye his kingdom, and
these things shall be added unto you. Fear not, little
flock ; for it is your Father's good pleasure to give you
the kingdom. Sell that ye have, and give alms ; make
for yourselves purses which wax not old, a treasure in
the heavens that faileth not, where no thief draweth
near, nor moth destroyeth. For where your treasure is,
there will your heart be also.*

St. Luke vi. 37–42.

And judge not, and ye shall not be judged : and
condemn not, and ye shall not be condemned : release,
and ye shall be released : give, and it shall be given
unto you ; good measure, pressed down, shaken
together, running over, shall they give into your
bosom. For with what measure ye mete it shall be
measured to you again.

And he spake also a parable unto them, Can the
blind guide the blind ? shall they not both fall into a
pit ? The disciple is not above his master : but
every one when he is perfected shall be as his master.
And why beholdest thou the mote that is in thy
brother's eye, but considerest not the beam that is
in thine own eye ? Or how canst thou say to thy
brother, Brother, let me cast out the mote that is in
thine eye, when thou thyself beholdest not the beam
that is in thine own eye ? Thou hypocrite, cast out
first the beam out of thine own eye, and then shalt
thou see clearly to cast out the mote that is in thy
brother's eye.

St. Luke xi. 9–13.

*And I say unto you, Ask, and it shall be given you ;
seek, and ye shall find ; knock, and it shall be opened
unto you. For every one that asketh receiveth ; and
he that seeketh findeth ; and to him that knocketh it*

which is in heaven give good things to them that
ask him ?   All things therefore whatsoever ye would
that men should do unto you, even so do ye also unto
them : for this is the law and the prophets.

Enter ye in by the narrow gate : for wide is the
gate, and broad is the way, that leadeth to destruction, and many be they that enter in thereby.   For
narrow is the gate, and straitened the way, that
leadeth unto life, and few be they that find it.

Beware of false prophets, which come to you in
sheep's clothing, but inwardly are ravening wolves.
By their fruits ye shall know them.   Do men gather
grapes of thorns, or figs of thistles ?   Even so every
good tree bringeth forth good fruit ; but the corrupt
tree bringeth forth evil fruit.   A good tree cannot
bring forth evil fruit, neither can a corrupt tree bring
forth good fruit.   Every tree that bringeth not forth
good fruit is hewn down, and cast into the fire.
Therefore by their fruits ye shall know them.   Not
every one that saith unto me, Lord, Lord, shall
enter into the kingdom of heaven ; but he that
doeth the will of my Father which is in heaven.   Many
will say to me in that day, Lord, Lord, did we not
prophesy by thy name, and by thy name cast out
devils, and by thy name do many mighty works ?
And then will I profess unto them, I never knew you :
depart from me, ye that work iniquity.   Every one
therefore which heareth these words of mine, and
doeth them, shall be likened unto a wise man, which
built his house upon the rock : and the rain descended,
and the floods came, and the winds blew, and beat
upon that house ; and it fell not : for it was founded
upon the rock.   And every one that heareth these
words of mine, and doeth them not, shall be likened
unto a foolish man, which built his house upon the
sand : and the rain descended, and the floods came,
and the winds blew, and smote upon that house ;
and it fell : and great was the fall thereof.

And it came to pass, when Jesus ended these

*shall be opened.   And of which of you that is a father
shall his son ask a loaf, and he give him a stone ? or a
fish, and he for a fish give him a serpent ?   Or if he
shall ask an egg, will he give him a scorpion ?   If ye
then, being evil, know how to give good gifts unto your
children, how much more shall your heavenly Father
give the Holy Spirit to them that ask him ?*

xiii. 24–27.

*Strive to enter in by the narrow door : for many, I
say unto you, shall seek to enter in, and shall not be
able.   When once the master of the house is risen up,
and hath shut to the door, and ye begin to stand without,
and to knock at the door, saying, Lord, open to us ; and
he shall answer and say to you, I know you not whence
ye are ; then shall ye begin to say, We did eat and
drink in thy presence, and thou didst teach in our
streets ; and he shall say, I tell you, I know not whence
ye are ; depart from me, all ye workers of iniquity.*

vi. 43–49.

For there is no good tree that bringeth forth
corrupt fruit ; nor again a corrupt tree that bringeth
forth good fruit.   For each tree is known by its own
fruit.   For of thorns men do not gather figs, nor of
a bramble bush gather they grapes.   The good man
out of the good treasure of his heart bringeth forth
that which is good ; and the evil man out of the evil
treasure bringeth forth that which is evil : for out
of the abundance of the heart his mouth speaketh.

And why call ye me, Lord, Lord, and do not the
things which I say ?   Every one that cometh unto
me, and heareth my words, and doeth them, I will
show you to whom he is like : he is like a man building a house, who digged and went deep, and laid a
foundation upon the rock : and when a flood arose,
the stream brake against that house, and could not

words, the multitudes were astonished at his teaching : for he taught them as one having authority, and not as their scribes.

And when he was come down from the mountain, great multitudes followed him.

shake it : because it had been well builded.   But he
that heareth, and doeth not, is like a man that built
a house upon the earth without a foundation ; against
which the stream brake, and straightway it fell in ;
and the ruin of that house was great.

APPENDIX II

IT has been noticed above in the exposition of St. Matt. v. 21–48 that different moral principles are brought out by our Lord in His treatment of the different commandments. Thus in His treatment of Commandment VI (vv. 21–24) the moral requirement is deepened in its application below the act to the words of the lips and the thoughts of the heart. In the treatment of Commandment VII, not only is the outward scope of the sin of adultery enlarged by a stricter law of marriage (vv. 31–32), but also the deliberate intention of sin is shown to be, without proceeding further, the moral equivalent of the outward act of sin [1] (vv. 27–28); from the recognition of which principle there follows the need of an augmented moral discipline (vv. 29–30). In the treatment of Commandment III, starting from the prohibition to violate any oath made in the name of Jehovah (v. 33), our Lord augments the prohibition by forbidding oaths generally (vv. 34–36), and turns the requirement from the negative to the positive and

---

[1] This is a higher moral principle than that Jewish method of "making a fence to the law," which is expressed in the *Didachè* 3. "Be not prone to anger, *for anger leads to murder* . . . Be not lustful, *for lust leads to fornication*." The wrong condition of the will is, according to our Lord, itself the evil, apart from what it may lead to. What is needed is not merely outward respectability or conformity, but a right spirit.

from the occasional to the universal (v. 37), by
simply enjoining truthfulness or sincerity in all
utterances.

In His treatment of the prohibition of unrestricted
revenge (vv. 38–42), and the principle of limited love
(vv. 43–48), the same two principles emerge—the
transition from negation or prohibition of evil to
injunction of positive good, and from the partial or
limited duty to the universal and perfect.

These principles admit of general application to
each of the commandments.   Thus—

I. *Thou shalt have none other gods before* [or *beside*]
me.   Whatever be the original limitation of this
precept, it becomes, and indeed in the teaching of
psalmist and prophet which prepared for the Christ
had already become, a universal injunction upon
men to recognize the one true God in every faculty
of their being, in every act and moment of their
lives.   "Thou shalt love the Lord thy God with all
thy heart (or will), with all thy soul (i.e. with thy
whole sum of faculties), with all thy mind (or intelligence), and with all thy strength (i.e. with a vigorous
and active service)."   This includes (1) the recognition of God's supremacy and fatherhood; the putting
Him first in all things; the acknowledgement that
our life with all its faculties is a trust to be made the
best of, for His honour : (2) humility, considered as
the recognition that we are utterly dependent upon
God ; that our only wisdom and happiness lie in
correspondence with Him ; that any claim of independence of God, or vanity on account of His gifts
entrusted to us, is not only wickedness but folly : [1]
(3) the glad acceptance of His disclosure of Himself
as Father, Son, and Spirit ; the acknowledgement
and public confession of His name both in speech,
conduct and worship.

[1] Humility both towards God and towards our fellow-
men is simply the recognition of the truth about ourselves.

II. *Thou shalt not make unto thee a graven image, etc.* This negative commandment becomes the positive injunction to worship God aright, as He has revealed Himself to us, " in spirit and in truth "; or in other words, according to the spirit of the Lord's Prayer and of the Eucharist, which are of Christ's institution ; or in the spirit of His own worship. This involves earnestness and effort of will in prayer : reasonable method, and use of the body with its faculties or instruments : the action of the intelligence meditating on the word of God so that we may have right ideas about God : systematic prayer for others—the Church, humanity, various classes and individuals—as well as for ourselves: public prayer and private : adoration and thanksgiving, as well as making requests—i.e. a life of worship of which the two hinges are the Eucharist (St. Luke xxii. 19) and secret prayer (St. Matt. vi. 6). This positive injunction involves negatives. Thus though the old prohibition to make any visible representation of God is modified by His incarnation, it still remains a duty which the Church has often neglected to guard against idolatry. It is idolatry to let our worship (1) be directed towards persons lower than God, as mediators, because they seem easier to approach and less awful ; or (2) rest upon circumscribed objects so as to imperil the omnipresence of God ; or (3) be moulded by false conceptions of God, as when the worth of prayer is estimated by the place where it is offered, or by some measure of length, contrary to the principles expressed in St. John iv. 21 ff., St. Matt. vi. 7.

III. *Thou shalt not take the name of the Lord thy God in vain.* This limited prohibition of perjury becomes the positive and universal injunction of truthfulness, i.e. the injunction to live and therefore to speak as in God's presence, so that our words represent the reality, so far as we can know it, whether those words be promises, or statements (*a*) personal,

(b) historical or scientific. This duty of truthfulness extends into all regions of life, political, commercial, controversial, as well as the private and domestic sphere, i.e. we are never justified in deceiving others for our own interest or that of our Church or party.[1]

This commandment, as deepened by our Lord, also prohibits all other kinds of speech which by their character ignore the reverence we owe to an omnipresent God, i.e. blasphemous or unmeaning

[1] It can hardly, however, be denied that there are rare cases where untruthfulness in word becomes a duty owing to the social evil which verbal truthfulness would involve. Thus almost all men would think it right to lie to a would-be murderer in order to save a life. I twice heard the late Master of Balliol, who had great moral common sense, in answer to the question what he would do in such a case, reply : " I suppose I should tell the lie, but I had rather not think about it beforehand or justify it afterwards." This is the best answer in regard to such quite abnormal cases. But there are certain more normal cases where professional reserve involves something approaching untruthfulness. The lawyer, doctor, or Cabinet Minister may be asked a question which ought not to be asked, and have no alternative but to give some more or less misleading answer, or in effect disclose (even by silence or refusal to answer) a professional secret. The " seal of the confessional " —imposed on the clergy (with a gradually increasing stringency) by the general law of the Church and by the Anglican canons of 1603 (c. 113)—is an intensified case of such professional obligation of secrecy. In such cases the possible moral evil is reduced to a minimum if society recognizes that what is known under a " seal," sacramental or professional, is not included in the knowledge which is recognized in social life. I have written the above because if there are circumstances, however rare, where a man would not act on the ordinary obligation of candid speech he had better give general public notice of it. But I cannot feel satisfied with the reasonings of moralists, Jesuit, Anglican or Protestant, about the morality of the matter. E.g. Newman Smyth, *Christian Ethics* (Clark, Edin. 1892), pp. 388 ff.

oaths and expressions derogatory to God's honour, irreverent or "foolish talking and jesting which are not convenient," etc.

IV. *Remember the sabbath day, to keep it holy. Six days shalt thou labour, and do all thy work : but the seventh day is a sabbath unto the Lord thy God : in it thou shalt not do any work, thou, nor thy son, nor thy daughter, nor thy manservant, nor thy maidservant, nor thy cattle, nor thy stranger that is within thy gates : for in six days the Lord made heaven and earth, the sea, and all that in them is, and rested the seventh day : wherefore the Lord blessed the sabbath day, and hallowed it.*

This commandment lays down three laws for human life.

1. The law of work, which—though the kinds of work are various, as of body, mind, character, spirit, suffering—lies upon all men alike. "If any man will not work, neither let him eat."

2. The law of rest, like God's rest. God works, as in creation, redemption, the establishment of the kingdom ; and then rests in contemplation of His finished work ; see Gen. i. 31, Matt. iii. 17, Rev. xxi. 2 : or, as otherwise stated by our Lord (St. John v. 17), God works continually and yet rests in working, as is exemplified in our Lord ' semper agens, semper quietus." Thus man is to share God's rest, by resting in God (Ps. cxxvii), and the sabbath was intended to help to this end. The sabbath however was a day of rest from physical labour, which only secondarily became a day of worship. The Christian Lord's day, on the other hand, was originally a day of worship, which became secondarily a day of rest from labour. The primary object of Sunday is that men by taking time and thought for worship should learn the true rest, which is rest in God. The secondary object is that all men equally should have the opportunity for physical rest and recreation. All questions as to Sunday observance are to be

judged by their relation to those two objects in their right order.

3. The law of fellowship. This fellowship of all men (and even of men with beasts) is developed in the New Testament into the principle that each man has a right to equal consideration, that each man counts for one, and nobody for more than one. Cp. above, p. 182.

V. *Honour thy father and thy mother : that thy days may be long upon the land which the Lord thy God giveth thee.* By this " commandment with promise " honour to parents, which is the principle of family life, is made also the basis of national prosperity (cf. Deut. v. 16). It is enlarged in all the " wise sayings " of the Book of Proverbs about family life. It receives its completion in the principle of mutual duty between parents and children, husbands and wives, masters and servants, which are enunciated in such passages as Eph. v. 22—vi. 9 ; Col. iii. 18—iv. 1. It receives a natural extension, so as to include the whole principle of mutual subordination in Church and State : cf. Hebr. xiii. 17 ; Rom. xiii ; 1 Pet. ii. 13—iii. 7. It involves towards the Church the duty, not only of loyal obedience, but of generous support. " Give to thy mother what thou wouldst allow to ev'ry corporation."

VI. *Thou shalt do no murder.* This commandment is developed by our Lord so as to prohibit hatred or contempt in thought and word as well as in deed. Translated from the negative into the positive it becomes an injunction to do all that lies in one's power to promote the life of others, physically and spiritually—to " love thy neighbour as thyself "—and to do this with a good will even towards enemies.

VII. *Thou shalt not commit adultery.* Our Lord deals with this commandment partly by an increased strictness with regard to the marriage law which brings under the head of adultery a number of re-marriages after divorce hitherto tolerated under the

Jewish system ; partly by making the indulged intention to sin equally guilty with the sin itself. On another occasion our Lord gives " adulteries, fornications, lasciviousness," a conspicuous place among the sins which " proceed out of the heart " or " from within," as though to emphasize the necessity in regard to this class of sins in particular of cleansing the inner springs of action and feeling. If we make the injunction positive and general instead of negative and partial, we arrive at the " law of liberty," the duty of subordinating the flesh to the spirit, in respect of eating and drinking, as well as of the sexual passions ; and the necessity of self-discipline or fasting as a means to that end (see above, pp. 120 f.).

VIII. *Thou shalt not steal*, converted from the negative into the positive, becomes " Thou shalt labour, working with thine hands the thing that is good, that thou mayest have to give to him that needeth." [1] It is, in another form, the loving one's neighbour as oneself : the having the same care for his goods as for one's own : the same anxiety that he should have proper wages for labour as oneself. From the Christian point of view this commandment is broken, not only by stealing in the ordinary sense, but also (1) by fraudulent dealings in business or trade, whereby our fellow man receives for money given something less, or other, than he had a right to expect : (2) by " sweating " or requiring others to work for inadequate wages : (3) by giving or receiving bribes or, in other ways, defrauding an employer of the best service of the employed : (4) by expecting others to work for us without doing our own fair share of work : (5) by neglecting or inadequately performing the duty of almsgiving. And in our generation we specially need reminding that association in " companies " leaves the moral responsibility for commercial dealings still resting on each member of

[1] Eph. iv. 28 ; 1 Tim. vi. 17, 18 ; James v. 4.

the company, at least in the form of a duty to vote
for directors who will have righteousness in view :
to discountenance all unrighteousness as far as
possible : to refuse gains for unrighteous dealing,
when known. In all cases the Christian must prefer
to suffer wrong rather than to do it.

IX. *Thou shalt not bear false witness against thy
neighbour.* This commandment, converted from the
negative—the prohibition of wilful slander—to the
positive, becomes an injunction to make the law of
love the motive of all our speech, with as tender a
regard to others' reputation as to our own. We
may have to speak painful truth against others, to
rebuke, to accuse, to punish, etc., but the motive of
all speech is to be a deliberate good will.

X. *Thou shalt not covet thy neighbour's house, etc.*
The ten commandments, as has been remarked, began
and ended with an injunction bearing not upon the
outward conduct, but upon the heart. This one
affords no discouragement to our vital instinct of
making the best of ourselves, but it bids us have
regard to what we can ascertain of the divine intention for ourselves. We are to realize God's purpose
for us, and to desire that every one else should do the
same. Thus this commandment prohibits envy or
jealousy at another's success or abilities : discontent
with what God has allowed us : ambition properly
so called, i.e. the desire to compass greatness, without
regard to the will of God. The New Testament
even tends to make us personally prefer the humbler
to the higher place, and obedience to authority. But,
on the other hand, it says all that is possible to encourage a " divine discontent " with the disorder
of the world, which is the work of evil wills resisting
the will of God, that sort of discontent which makes
a man a fellow-worker with Christ for the realization
of the kingdom of heaven.

I have thought this analysis of the ten commandments in their deepest principles, inadequate as it is, might be worth making, partly because I cannot feel altogether satisfied with such as are commonly current,[1] partly because the attempt to make such an analysis deepens in my own mind the conviction that if the ten commandments were not—as our Lord teaches us they were not—perfect, they were none the less, in the truest sense, " the word of God," for the moral education of His chosen people, and through them of the human race. Their principles are extraordinarily complete and suggestive, and there is no early moral legislation which seems to me to be even comparable to them.

[1] The account of our duty to God and our duty towards our neighbour in our Catechism is, when quoted correctly (" in that state of life into which it *shall* please God to call me ") and interpreted rightly (" betters " not meaning " those keeping carriages "), admirable, but of course very short.

APPENDIX III

ABOVE, in the text of the exposition, it has been maintained (1) that Christ, by a distinct act of legislation, prohibited divorce among His disciples in such sense as allows of remarriage, except in the case of the adultery of one of the parties, in which case He did not prohibit it ; but (2) that the Church law and tradition in England, as in the whole Western Church, maintains the absolute indissolubility of the marriage tie. Both propositions, however, are denied, and it is necessary to make some remarks upon the respective denials.

1. The present tendency of those who deny that Christ's words, as repeated on two occasions in St. Matthew's Gospel, allow the remarriage of the innocent party after divorce for adultery is—abandoning with good cause the older arguments (1) that πορνεία only applies to prenuptial sin : (2) that the words as quoted in St. Matthew were only intended to apply to the Jews—to lay stress upon the uncertainty of the text in St. Matt. xix where the words occur " and shall marry another." To this it may be replied (i) that it is strange to find people not generally recognized as very advanced textual critics going, in this single case, further than even Dr. Hort ventured to go, in maintaining the textual authority of the Vatican manuscript, which alone among the great uncials omits the clause ; (ii) that it would appear sufficiently obvious that the variation of the

text in this passage is due to assimilation to the similar passage in chapter v ; (iii) that it is not time to deprive people of the right to appeal to an accepted text until some trustworthy editors have been found to venture to remove it from its place ; (iv) that the sense remains the same in any case. For the text, as given in chapter v, or in chapter xix with the words " and shall marry another " omitted, yet carries the liberty to do so, see text given above, pp. 72, 73. Divorce, as understood by the Jews, meant divorce *a vinculo*, i.e. divorce with liberty of re-marriage. Is any sane man prepared to say that divorce, in the sense of separation of a wife from bed and board, without liberty of remarriage, is only permissible to a Christian when the wife has been adulterous ?

I do not think then that the obvious force of the passages in St. Matthew can be dissolved.

2. On the other hand, admitting all that can be said as to the difficulty, which is due to the historical relation of Church and State in England, of saying what is Church law pure and simple, it does seem to me that the Western law of divorce, as distinct from the Eastern, was accepted by the English Church and not only never repudiated, but at least assumed to be permanent in the Post-Reformation Canons. What has happened since then is (1) that the opinion of a great number of the best English divines and commentators on St. Matthew has been expressed in favour of allowing the remarriage of the " innocent party " after a divorce for adultery ; (2) that the Lambeth Conference of 1888 allowed such re-marriage ; (3) that statute law in England has recently allowed the remarriage of both innocent and guilty party.

But the Lambeth Conference only expresses the opinion (however weighty) of a gathering of Anglican bishops. It cannot legislate for the Church of England. And the legislation which has taken place

is purely civil legislation made from a civil point
of view and going beyond what the Lambeth
Conference would allow. And on such a matter as
marriage which lies at the heart of our religious life
it seems quite unreasonable to ask Christian people
to accept this, as authority sufficient to upset an
ancient practice of the Church.

Granted then (1) that Christ did not prohibit [1]
the remarriage of an innocent party after a divorce
for adultery, (2) that the unaltered Church law of
England does prohibit it, it seems to me that the
best course is *not*, at least in the present state of
Church feeling, to alter the Church law on the matter,
up to the point which Christ allows, by getting leave
for Convocation to make a new Canon—though this
would be a course to which no one could take just
exception—but to retain and observe the Church
law, allowing no remarriage with the rites of the
Church, but simply leaving it to bishops to act on
the decision of the Lambeth Conference as far as
admission to communion is concerned.

This refusal to allow remarriage in churches may
involve some collision with statute law till an equit-
able concession to our principles is accorded. But
the difficulty is not greater than has been overcome
by a little resolution in the case of the Public Worship
Regulation Act. If in the process of the contro-
versy the institution of compulsory civil marriage
here in England, with the same publicity as in most
foreign countries, to be followed by a voluntary
religious ceremony, becomes a more likely event,
there would be a good many Churchmen who would
not regret it.

As regards the allowance of remarriage to the
innocent party after a divorce for adultery, it is

---

[1] It is perhaps hardly fair to say more than this.
Christ simply exempted a particular case from a general
prohibition, leaving the Church free in regard to it.

sometimes pointed out that it is only explicitly allowed by our Lord to the innocent *husband*. But it is, I submit, at least competent to the Church to interpret this in the more lenient sense as extending to the aggrieved wife also. It is more often urged that it is illogical to forbid to the guilty party what is allowed to the innocent—that if declared adultery dissolves the marriage tie for either, it does so for both. To this I should only reply that our Lord appears on the matter to be *legislating* rather than laying down a principle. His legislation covers the one exception but not (with any degree of clearness) the other. He appears to be sanctioning in the case of an innocent and deeply aggrieved person a dispensation which violates the logic of the marriage tie on grounds of equity : but this carries with it no necessary consequence of a similar dispensation in favour of the chief offender.

INDEXES

I. PERSONS AND AUTHORITIES CITED

II. SUBJECTS

III. TEXTS ELUCIDATED

IV. APHORISMS—" SEED THOUGHTS "

Atonement, must = redemption, 199

Attitude of others to us, 39
" On the whole we can determine men's attitude to us by our attitude to them "

Body and spirit must be treated together, 123

Care for health, 160
" We ought to be reasonably careful and to go boldly forward in the peace of God "

Church, the offer of the, 174–5

Comfort from God, 31

Conscience, 155
" Conscience is only a faculty for knowing God and His will. It is certain, unless it is educated, to give wrong information "

Cost of duty, 188

Dealing of God with us, 40–1

Duty to self, 114
" Our duty towards ourselves is, in a word, to make the best of ourselves "

God's dealings, 40–1, 85
" God dealt with men gradually "

Health, care for, 160

Helping others, 46
" You are to help men by being unlike them "

How to make people better, 106

Imperfection, God's treatment of, 55
" God does not despair of what is imperfect because it is imperfect. He views every institution (or person) not as it is, but as it is becoming "

" Judge not," 163, 168
" Make the best of everything and every person "
" From all sides you get as you give "

Law of Correspondence in prayer, 148

Law of Prayer, 149
" We must not ask that God will violate His general laws in our private interest "

Motive, real test of, 151

" Name of Christ," in the, 140, 142
" To pray in the name of Christ means to pray in such a way as represents Christ "

These Indexes the author owes to the kindness of the Rev. W. E. ASHDOWN.

Printed by Hazell, Watson & Viney, Ld., London and Aylesbury.

WORKS BY THE SAME AUTHOR

THE INCARNATION OF THE SON OF GOD.
BAMPTON LECTURES, 1891. *Cheap Edition.* Large Crown 8vo.
2s. 6d. net.

WHY WE CHRISTIANS BELIEVE IN CHRIST.
THE BAMPTON LECTURES. Shortened for Popular Use by the Rev.
T. C. FRY. Fcap. 8vo. 1s. net.

THE MISSION OF THE CHURCH. Four Lectures
delivered in the Cathedral Church of St. Asaph. Crown 8vo. 2s. 6d.

DISSERTATIONS ON SUBJECTS CONNECTED
WITH THE INCARNATION. *Cheap Edition.* Large Crown
8vo. 2s. 6d. net.

THE BODY OF CHRIST. An Enquiry into the Institution
and Doctrine of the Holy Communion. *Fourth Edition.* With a
New Introduction. Crown 8vo. 2s. 6d. net.

THE SERMON ON THE MOUNT. A Practical Explanation. Crown 8vo. 2s. 6d. net. Also 1s. net and 6d. net.

EPISTLE TO THE EPHESIANS. A Practical Exposition.
Crown 8vo. 2s. 6d. net.

EPISTLE TO THE ROMANS. A Practical Exposition.
2 Vols. Crown 8vo. 2s. 6d. net each.

THE NEW THEOLOGY AND THE OLD RELI-
GION. Being Eight Lectures, together with Five Sermons. Crown
8vo. 5s. net.

SPIRITUAL EFFICIENCY. The Primary Charge delivered
at his Visitation to the Clergy and Churchwardens of his Diocese,
Worcester, 1904. Demy 8vo. In Paper Covers. 1s. net.

THE PERMANENT CREED AND THE CHRIS-
TIAN IDEA OF SIN. Two Sermons preached before the Univer-
sity of Oxford. Large Crown 8vo. Paper Covers. 6d. net.

OBJECTIONS TO THE EDUCATION BILL 1906,
IN PRINCIPLE AND IN DETAIL. Large Crown 8vo. Paper
Covers. 2d. net.

EDITED BY BISHOP GORE

LUX MUNDI. A Series of Studies in the Religion of the Incarnation. By VARIOUS WRITERS. *Cheap Edition.* Large Crown 8vo.
2s. 6d. net.

ESSAYS ON CHURCH REFORM. By NUMEROUS
WRITERS. Crown 8vo. *Cheap Edition.* 5s. net.

MURRAY'S
SHILLING LIBRARY

Crown 8vo. Cloth, 1/= net each

A NATURALIST ON THE RIVER AMAZON
A Record of Adventures, Habits of Animals, Sketches
of Brazilian and Indian Life, and Aspects of Nature
under the Equator, during Eleven Years of Travel.
By H. W. BATES, F.R.S. Numerous Illustrations.

A LADY'S LIFE IN THE ROCKY MOUNTAINS
By Mrs. BISHOP (ISABELLA BIRD). With Illustrations.

DEEDS OF NAVAL DARING;
or, ANECDOTES OF THE BRITISH NAVY. By
EDWARD GIFFARD.

THE PAINTERS OF FLORENCE
From the 13th to the 16th Centuries. By JULIA
CARTWRIGHT (Mrs. ADY). With Illustrations.

SELF=HELP
With Illustrations of Conduct and Perseverance. By
SAMUEL SMILES. With Portrait.

THE LIFE OF DAVID LIVINGSTONE
By WILLIAM GARDEN BLAIKIE. With Portrait.

SINAI AND PALESTINE
In connection with their History. By the late Dean
STANLEY. With Maps.

WORKS BY A. C. BENSON

THE THREAD OF GOLD

THE HOUSE OF QUIET. An Autobiography.